Environmental Performance Reviews

Ireland

OECD

ORGANISATION FOR ECONOMIC CO-OPERATION AND DEVELOPMENT

ORGANISATION FOR ECONOMIC CO-OPERATION AND DEVELOPMENT

Pursuant to Article 1 of the Convention signed in Paris on 14th December 1960, and which came into force on 30th September 1961, the Organisation for Economic Co-operation and Development (OECD) shall promote policies designed:

- to achieve the highest sustainable economic growth and employment and a rising standard of living in Member countries, while maintaining financial stability, and thus to contribute to the development of the world economy;
- to contribute to sound economic expansion in Member as well as non-member countries in the process of economic development; and
- to contribute to the expansion of world trade on a multilateral, non-discriminatory basis in accordance with international obligations.

The original Member countries of the OECD are Austria, Belgium, Canada, Denmark, France, Germany, Greece, Iceland, Ireland, Italy, Luxembourg, the Netherlands, Norway, Portugal, Spain, Sweden, Switzerland, Turkey, the United Kingdom and the United States. The following countries became Members subsequently through accession at the dates indicated hereafter: Japan (28th April 1964), Finland (28th January 1969), Australia (7th June 1971), New Zealand (29th May 1973), Mexico (18th May 1994), the Czech Republic (21st December 1995), Hungary (7th May 1996), Poland (22nd November 1996) and Korea (12th December 1996). The Commission of the European Communities takes part in the work of the OECD (Article 13 of the OECD Convention).

Publié en français sous le titre :
EXAMENS DES PERFORMANCES ENVIRONNEMENTALES
IRLANDE

FOREWORD

The principal aim of the OECD's environmental performance reviews is to help *Member countries improve their individual and collective performances in environmental management*. The primary goals for this programme are:

- to help *individual governments* assess progress by establishing baseline conditions, trends, policy commitments, institutional arrangements and routine capabilities for carrying out national evaluations;

- to promote environmental improvements and a continuous policy *dialogue among Member countries*, through a peer review process and by the transfer of information on policies, approaches and experiences of reviewed countries; and

- to stimulate *greater accountability* from Member countries' governments towards public opinion within developed countries and beyond.

Programme efforts are directed at *promoting sustainable development*, with emphasis on developments in domestic and international environmental policy, as well as on the integration of economic and environmental decision-making.

Environmental performance is assessed with regard to the degree of achievement of *domestic objectives and international commitments*. Such objectives and commitments may be broad aims, specific qualitative goals, precise quantitative targets or a commitment to a set of measures to be taken. Assessment of environmental performance is also placed within the context of historical environmental records, the present state of the environment, the physical endowment of the country in natural resources, its economic conditions and demographic trends.

These systematic, independent and periodic reviews are organised and conducted in a way similar to the OECD's economic reviews. The report is peer-reviewed by the Working Party on Environmental Performance, composed of officials from Member countries who have responsibility for national environmental policy development and implementation and a broad competence recognised at national and international levels. The conclusions and recommendations of the report are approved by the Working Party.

Joke Waller-Hunter
Director
Environment Directorate

GENERAL INTRODUCTION

This review of Ireland environmental performance *examines results to date* in the light of domestic objectives and international commitments. Four countries assisted with this review: New Zealand, Norway, Portugal and the United States.

The report is organised in three parts according to the strategic goals identified by OECD Environment Ministers:

- Part I is entitled "Pollution Prevention and Control" and focuses on water, air and waste management;
- Part II is entitled "Integration of Policies" and focuses on institutional aspects and on how policies concerning economics and transport are integrated with environmental policies;
- Part III is entitled "Co-operation with the International Community" and focuses on international environmental topics concerning Ireland.

The OECD extends its most sincere thanks to all those who helped in the course of this review, and especially to the examining countries (New Zealand, Norway, Portugal and the United States) and their experts. The OECD is particularly indebted to the Government of Ireland for its co-operation in expediting the provision of information and the organisation of the experts' mission to Ireland, and in facilitating contacts with many individuals both inside and outside administrative and governmental structures of the country.

The OECD Working Party on Environmental Performance conducted the review at its meeting on 3-5 July 2000 and approved its conclusions and recommendations. This report is published under the authority of the Secretary-General of the OECD.

OUTLINE OF THE REPORT

Part I

POLLUTION PREVENTION AND CONTROL

Part II

INTEGRATION OF POLICIES

Part III

CO-OPERATION WITH THE INTERNATIONAL COMMUNITY

DETAILED TABLE OF CONTENTS

LIST OF FIGURES AND TABLES

ABBREVIATIONS AND SIGNS

Abbreviations

AAMA	American Automobile Manufacturers Association
ACPH	Advisory Committee on Pollution by Hydrocarbons and other harmful substances discharged at sea (EU)
BATNEEC	Best available techniques not entailing excessive cost
BNM	Bord na Móna (peat-harvesting company)
BOD	Biochemical oxygen demand
BTX	Benzene, toluene and xylenes
CAP	Common Agricultural Policy (EU)
cc	Cubic centimetres
CFCs	Chlorofluorocarbons
CFPS	Control of Farmyard Pollution Scheme
CH_4	Methane
CIE	Coras Iompair Eireann (the State Transport Company)
CITES	Convention on International Trade in Endangered Species of Wild Fauna and Flora
CNG	Compressed natural gas
CO	Carbon monoxide
CO_2	Carbon dioxide
CSF	Community Support Framework
DAC	Development Assistance Committee, OECD
DAHGI	Department of Arts, Heritage, Gaeltacht and the Islands
DART	Dublin Area Rapid Transit
DDDA	Dublin Docklands Development Authority
DO	Dissolved oxygen
DOELG	Department of the Environment and Local Government
DPE	Department of Public Enterprise
DTI	Dublin Transportation Initiative
EAP	Environment Action Programme
EEC	European Economic Community
EIA	Environmental impact assessment
EIS	Environmental impact statement
EMAS	Eco-Management and Audit Scheme (EU)
EMEP	Environmental Monitoring and Evaluation Programme
EMS	Environmental Management System
ENFO	National environmental information centre
EPA	Environmental Protection Agency
EQO	Environmental Quality Objective(s)
ERRA	European Recovery and Recycling Association
ESA	Environmentally Sensitive Area
ESB	Electricity Supply Board
ESRI	Economic and Social Research Institute
EUR	Euro

FAO	Food and Agriculture Organisation
FDI	Foreign direct investment
FIP	Farm Improvement Programme
GEF	Global Environment Facility
GHG	Greenhouse gas(es)
GWP	Global warming potential
HNS	Hazardous and noxious substances
IEA	International Energy Agency
IEC	Irish Energy Centre
IFSC	International Financial Services Centre
IMES	Irish Marine Emergency Services
IMO	International Maritime Organisation
IPC	Integrated Pollution Control
IRF	International Road Federation
ISO	International Organisation for Standardisation
IWSA	International Water Supply Association
kt	Kilotonne
LPG	Liquified petroleum gas
MARPOL	International Convention for the Prevention of Pollution from Ships
Mt	Million tonnes
Mtoe	Million tonnes of oil equivalent
MW	Megawatt
N_2O	Nitrous oxide
NCT	National Car Test
NEA	Nuclear Energy Agency
NGO	Non-governmental organisation
NHA	Natural Heritage Area
NO_x	Nitrogen oxides
NPK	Nitrogen phosphorous potassium
NRA	National Roads Authority
NSS	National Spatial Strategy
O_3	Ozone
ODA	Official development assistance
ODS	Ozone depleting substance(s)
OP	Operational Programme
OPP	Operational Programme on Peripherality
OPT	Operational Programme for Transport
OSPAR	Convention for the Protection of the Marine Environment of the North-East Atlantic
PAC	Pollution abatement and control
PM_{10}	Particulate matter < 10 μm in diameter
PPP	Purchasing power parity
QBC	Quality bus corridor
REPS	Rural Environmental Protection Scheme
RON	Research octane number
SAC	Special Area of Conservation
SCATS	Computerised traffic management system
SO_x	Sulphur oxides
SO_2	Sulphur dioxide
SPA	Special Protection Area

TAC	Total Allowable Catch
TBT	Tributyltin tin
TFC	Total final energy consumption
THERMIE	EU energy conservation programme
toe	Tonne of oil equivalent
TPES	Total primary energy supply
UNCED	UN Conference on Environment and Development
UNCSD	UN Commission on Sustainable Development
UNDP	UN Development Programme
UNEP	UN Environment Programme
USD	United States dollar
VAT	Value added tax
VOCs	Volatile organic compounds
VRT	Vehicle registration tax
WHO	World Health Organisation
WMP	Waste management plan(s)
WTO	World Trade Organisation

Signs

The following signs are used in Figures and Tables:
.. : not available
− : nil or negligible
. : decimal point

Country Aggregates

OECD Europe: All European Member countries of the OECD, i.e. countries of the European Union plus the Czech Republic, Hungary, Iceland, Norway, Poland, Switzerland and Turkey.
OECD: The countries of OECD Europe plus Australia, Canada, Japan, Korea, Mexico, New Zealand and the United States.
Country aggregates may include Secretariat estimates.
The sign * indicates that only western Germany is included.
The sign ** indicates that not all countries are included.

Currency

Monetary unit: pound (IEP)
On average in 1998, IEP 0.703 = USD 1

Cut-off Date

This report is based on information and data available up to December 1999.

LIST OF TEAM MEMBERS

Mr. Gunnar Farestveit	Expert from reviewing country: Norway
Mr. Thomas Kelly	Expert from reviewing country: United States
Mr. Pedro Nunes Liberato	Expert from reviewing country: Portugal
Mr. Eric Pyle	Expert from reviewing country: New Zealand
Mr. Christian Avérous	OECD Secretariat
Mr. Gérard Bonnis	OECD Secretariat
Mrs. Martha Heitzmann	OECD Secretariat
Mr. Heino Von Meyer	OECD Secretariat
Mr. Lucien Chabason	OECD Secretariat (Consultant)
Mr. Henri Smets	OECD Secretariat (Consultant)

CONCLUSIONS AND RECOMMENDATIONS*

Ireland has achieved remarkable economic performance in recent years: its GDP has grown by 9% annually since 1994, and its GDP per capita now surpasses the EU average. This has been made possible, inter alia, by a large inflow of *foreign direct investment* (2% of GDP annually) and considerable *EU net transfers* (in the range of 3-4% of GDP annually). With relatively low average population density, Ireland is experiencing rapid *suburbanisation* and population growth.

The new Irish economy (a large share of which is now made of the booming electronics and pharmaceuticals industries) is less energy and material intensive per unit of GDP than it was several years ago. However, absolute pressures on the environment have continued to increase, even if less rapidly than GDP. Ireland continues to face *many environmental challenges*, in particular controlling air emissions from transport and energy production, reducing pollution loading to water from municipal and agricultural sources, and improving waste management and nature protection. These challenges largely reflect insufficient environmental infrastructure, together with changes in consumption patterns associated with recent increases in per capita income. This makes it all the more necessary for Ireland to: i) further implement environmental policies and strengthen environmental infrastructure; ii) better integrate environmental concerns into economic decisions; and iii) reinforce international environmental co-operation.

This OECD report establishes a baseline for assessing future environmental progress and examines Ireland's environmental performance, i.e. the extent to which its *domestic objectives and international commitments* are being met, based on environmental effectiveness and economic efficiency criteria. A number of recommendations are put forward that could contribute to strengthening the country's environmental performance.

1. Implementing Environmental Policies

Ireland generally has *good environmental quality*. Thanks to its environmental policies and to the *"new economy"*, energy and material intensities fell in the 1990s. However, despite progress in some areas, particularly with regard to reducing emissions and effluents from industry, *pollution intensities are often high* compared to those in other European countries. Major challenges remain con-

---

* Conclusions and Recommendations reviewed and approved by the Working Party on Environmental Performance at its meeting on 4 July 2000.

---

cerning environmental pressures from energy production and agriculture, in particular from intensive livestock rearing. Pressures from municipal waste water are gradually decreasing with progress in waste water treatment, but they remain high. There are growing problems relating to changes in *consumption patterns*: for example, waste generation, transport and urban sprawl, particularly in the Dublin and Cork areas. To achieve higher environmental performance, Ireland will need to implement its environmental policies in a more cost-effective way. Due to insufficient investments in the past and requirements relating to new populations and urban development, it should increase its financial efforts to build a full-fledged modern environmental infrastructure.

Improving the cost-effectiveness of environmental policies and strengthening environmental infrastructure

Ireland has a *modern and coherent body of environmental law*. EU environmental law is fully transposed in national law. Most environmental legislation is less than ten years old; the new Planning and Development Bill consolidates physical planning legislation since 1963 and substantially updates strategic spatial planning at regional and local levels. The *Environmental Protection Agency (EPA)* plays an effective role in implementing environmental policy and monitoring performance, particularly through *Integrated Pollution Control (IPC)* for large industrial plants. Nevertheless, the EPA should have a more prominent role in licensing by local authorities and capacity building at the local level. Local authorities are responsible for managing municipal waste, water supply and waste water collection and treatment. For investment purposes they depend to a very large extent upon financing channelled by the Department of Environment and Local Government (DOELG), whether the funds come from European sources or national taxpayers. Up until now, Ireland has made only limited use of *economic instruments* to address pollution issues. Eliminating *water charges* for households was a step in the wrong direction. However, Ireland is progressively implementing a comprehensive charging system in respect of non-residential users. In a period of substantial investment in housing construction, water meters should be installed on new dwellings. Proposals for an increase in energy taxation, balanced by reductions in social charges, have been studied but not yet applied.

In the 1990s, Ireland launched *investment programmes* to build waste water collection and treatment facilities with a large share of EU support. Some time will be required to complete these programmes. As important investments in water supply, waste water treatment, waste treatment and air pollution control are still needed, Ireland should step up its national environmental investment effort. Environmental *operating expenditure* will also grow. In the 1990s, *environmental expenditure* (i.e. pollution abatement and control expenditure, together with that on water supply and nature protection) increased but did not exceed 1% of GDP.

Pollution abatement and control expenditure represents 0.6% of GDP, less than in most other OECD countries. Since *EU support* will progressively be phased out as a consequence of its economic performance, Ireland must prepare for a much more significant public and private financial effort with regard to environmental investment and management. Even if the Irish budget situation has improved, environmental expenditure will increasingly need to be covered by *charges* levied on polluters and resource users. Recent public-private partnerships in water services (e.g. build-operate-transfer projects) are steps in this direction.

In the 1990s, Ireland renovated its *environmental monitoring and reporting capacity* (e.g. State of the Environment reports, environmental indicators) and set up effective arrangements to translate into practice *public access to environmental information* (e.g. access to licenses, EIA processes and courts). The national environmental information centre *(ENFO)* provides valuable free access to a wide range of environment related information and is particularly active in environmental education.

It is *recommended* to:

- extend the positive experiences of the *IPC licensing* scheme to a number of other activities not yet covered;
- foster co-operation between *EPA and local authorities* in licensing and enforcement, e.g. through training and capacity building;
- extend the use of *economic instruments* that help inform polluters and resource users of the true costs of their activities;
- make the introduction of *revenue neutral eco-taxation* a subject in the new partnership agreement among the social partners;
- prepare for increased national *financing* of environmental expenditure, given the need for higher *investments* in water supply, waste water treatment, waste management facilities and air pollution control, likely increases in current expenditure, and the planned reduction of EU support;
- extend the range of environmental projects using *public-private partnerships*.

Water

Ireland has a well-developed system for monitoring water quality in rivers, lakes, groundwater and marine bathing water; data indicate that the state of *Irish water quality* is generally satisfactory. The institutional and legal systems, the latter influenced by EU legislation, address national major water management challenges. During a decade of rapid economic growth, Ireland has taken the measure of the water challenge it faces. A large programme of investment in water supply and waste water treatment put in place in the 1990s is progressing;

© OECD 2000

between 1994 and 1999, this programme benefited from large EU support. A number of farmers are required to adopt *nutrient management plans*. They receive direct payments as part of the Rural Environmental Protection Scheme (REPS) to support water quality protection measures. Integrated Pollution Control, implemented under the responsibility of the Environmental Protection Agency, includes licensing of waste water discharges from large industrial facilities. Efforts are being made to improve co-ordination among the various institutions involved in water management, in particular by promoting *water basin management*. Flood prevention schemes are well-maintained.

Since systematic records began to be kept in the early 1970s, there has been a substantial decline in water quality in Ireland's rivers and streams. This is nowadays largely attributable to *increased nutrients from crop and livestock production*. There are still "black spot" areas near *urban centres* that lack facilities to provide advanced urban waste water treatment. Improved enforcement of regulations and implementation of planning schemes are needed, especially in rural areas. The ecological management of water bodies should also be improved. *Leakage from water supply systems* accounts for as much as 45% of the water in distribution systems in some urban areas. *Drinking water quality* in rural areas is variable: up to 400 000 people may receive drinking water of substandard quality. Control of water pollution and of public water supply is supervised by the DOELG, which should facilitate *consolidation of the various pieces of water legislation*. *Household water charges* were discontinued in 1997, but charges applying to industrial and commercial establishments have not been abolished. Local authorities' expenditure on water services is mainly covered by the central government budget. To ultimately cover increasing capital and operational expenditures associated with water management, the User-Pays and Polluter-Pays Principles should be progressively applied. Public-private partnerships could also be encouraged, to address Ireland's challenging infrastructure deficit in the light of reduced EU funding. Overall, Ireland's water policies must meet very significant challenges. They are beginning to move towards better balancing of investment and operational management, better central and partenarial management, and autonomous and less EU-dependent financing.

It is *recommended* to:

- strengthen *catchment management* , with a greater role for river basin districts, and promote participatory approaches to the development of catchment plans;
- consolidate *water legislation* in order to increase accountability and clarify responsibilities;
- accelerate development of statutory nutrient management plans and by-laws for controlling *water pollution from agriculture*;

- develop *voluntary initiatives* aimed at water quality enhancement, such as contracts between fishermen and farmers to protect rivers;

- progressively apply the User-Pays and Polluter-Pays Principles to *water pricing policy* concerning both households and economic sectors, taking account of social and distributional concerns;

- promote greater *private sector* involvement in providing water services, technical expertise and access to financing;

- improve *drinking water quality* where necessary, especially regarding group water schemes;

- continue efforts to reduce *leakage* from water supplies to acceptable levels;

- develop ecosystem-based *environmental quality objectives* that are more holistic than current water management objectives, and that take into account nature conservation objectives;

- extend the highly effective *surface water monitoring system* to consider nature conservation issues, including habitat issues.

Air

Ambient air quality is high in small cities and rural areas and has improved significantly in large cities in regard to smoke, SO_x and lead. Since 1990, Ireland has successfully implemented a range of *regulatory measures* to improve urban air quality and reduce air emissions associated with transport and the housing sector. EU vehicle and fuel standards have been implemented. A ban on bituminous coal (instituted in Dublin in 1990, in Cork in 1995 and subsequently in ten other urban areas) has drastically reduced smoke emissions and improved urban air quality. Ireland achieved considerable energy intensity reductions in the 1990s, driven to a large extent by "dematerialisation" of the economy and increased market penetration by natural gas (21% of TPES). It uses some economic instruments to support air quality management objectives (e.g. in the transport sector).

Despite recent transformation of Irish industry, per capita air pollutant emissions (kg/per capita) remain considerably *higher than the OECD Europe average*: by 62% for SO_x, 20% for NO_x and 30% for CO_2. Despite recent progress, the emissions intensity (kg/USD 1 000) of the Irish economy exceeds the OECD Europe average by 25% for SO_x and 11% for CO_2. During the 1990s, Ireland did not take adequate steps to meet a number of *international commitments* to reduce emissions of certain pollutants, as envisaged in the Oslo and Sofia Protocols. Urgent measures are needed to improve emissions control, especially since Irish power stations continue to burn "dirty fuels". Some steps are being taken (e.g. decision to implement IPC licensing for all power plants by the end of 2002;

there is a voluntary cap on SO_x emissions from the power sector). Continued use of peat for power production, especially its continued subsidisation, should be re-evaluated. Peat's energy conversion efficiency is low, associated air emissions are rather high, and the environmental impact of peat harvesting is severe. Assuring that peat-fired plants are subject to IPC licensing from 2002, as scheduled, should be made a priority. Wider use of economic and fiscal measures to encourage use of *cleaner fuels* and *cleaner energy* should be given more consideration. In addition, several concerns about urban air quality (e.g. regarding PM_{10}, NO_x, VOCs and O_3) will require attention in the near future. Because of the rapid growth of its economy in recent years, Ireland confronts the challenge of using newly available resources to reduce emissions, notably in the face of greater energy demand, changing consumption patterns and increased commuting.

It is *recommended* to:

– develop and implement a *national plan to reduce air pollutant emissions*, to be co-ordinated with development plans for key sectors (e.g. transport, energy), and, inter alia, to identify cost-effective measures to reduce emissions of SO_x, NO_x, VOCs and GHGs;

– design and implement additional measures aimed at improving *energy efficiency* in industry and in the residential and commercial sectors, with consideration given to energy standards, pricing, and economic and fiscal incentives;

– continue to promote the use of *cleaner energy* (renewables, natural gas) compared with other sources of primary energy supply (coal, peat, oil);

– retrofit *power plants* with flue gas desulphurisation or denitrification equipment, to the extent that this is more cost-effective than creating incentives to use low-sulphur oil and coal; confirm a timetable for progressive phase-out of existing peat-fired power plants, especially those over ten years old;

– continue to implement the *IPC licensing* scheme and explore means to strengthen local authorities' monitoring and inspection capabilities, to ensure that facilities not licensed under the IPC scheme are adequately regulated;

– examine the environmental effectiveness and economic efficiency of *variable transport costs*, giving consideration to the use of higher taxation of motor vehicle fuels and the introduction of road-use pricing systems (e.g. use of tolls);

– further develop *monitoring* of ambient concentrations of PM_{10}, NO_x, VOCs and O_3, particularly in major cities.

Waste

Progress in waste management has been made in recent years, following enactment of a comprehensive *Waste Management Act* in 1996. The EPA has carried out detailed inventories of waste generation and landfill conditions; local authorities have prepared *waste management plans* providing for development of new waste infrastructure at the regional level. Industrial and municipal waste treatment and disposal facilities are now subject to IPC licensing by the EPA. The EPA has prepared a draft *National Hazardous Waste Management Plan*, currently at the public consultation stage. Ireland has ratified the Basel Convention on the Control of Transboundary Movement of Hazardous Wastes and their Disposal; it also conforms to the OECD Council Decision on Transfrontier Movements of Wastes Destined for Recovery Operations.

Waste management is the environmental area which, until recently, received *the least attention* in Ireland. Almost all municipal waste is disposed in *landfills*, most of which require to be upgraded to meet adequate environmental standards. *Recycling rates* are low and do not meet national targets. Recycling of construction and demolition waste needs to be encouraged. Neither regulatory nor economic measures are currently used to encourage recycling or reclamation of transport related wastes. More effort is needed to improve *waste prevention and reduction*, in particular through promoting development of low waste generation technologies. Efforts to increase separate collection of municipal waste should be pursued. Collection and disposal of end-of-life vehicles, used oil, tyres and batteries needs to be improved. It is estimated that 20% of the *hazardous waste* generated is not reported, of which a significant part is from the agricultural sector. Serious efforts are needed to increase the capacity to treat hazardous waste. Only one-half of municipal waste management costs are recovered through *waste charges* and landfill gate fees. The Polluter-Pays Principle should be applied more widely, in particular through applying household waste charges in all local authorities and, to the extent possible, linking them to the quantity of waste disposed. There is considerable scope for increased private sector involvement and investment in waste management.

It is *recommended* to:

— implement *waste management legislation* at the local level, in particular through completing the adoption of regional waste management plans;

— pursue efforts to close down or upgrade unsatisfactory *municipal landfills* as part of the development of a modern network of treatment and disposal facilities;

— promote *prevention of waste generation*, in particular by encouraging the uptake of low waste generation technologies;

- improve *recovery and recycling* of municipal and industrial wastes, including construction and demolition wastes, organic materials and transport wastes (used oil, lubricants and tyres);
- apply more fully the *Polluter-Pays Principle*, in particular through the general use of household waste charges and the proper pricing of landfill waste disposal, and promote private sector involvement in waste management;
- enhance *hazardous waste* treatment capacity (e.g. incineration), in particular by adopting and implementing the National Hazardous Waste Management Plan;
- further develop *producer responsibility* initiatives aimed at improving waste recovery performance.

2. Towards Sustainable Development

Integrating environmental concerns in economic decisions

During the 1990s, Ireland experienced i) steady economic growth (the highest among OECD countries); ii) structural change, with the rapid growth of, inter alia, information technology and biotechnology based industries; iii) improved income levels; and iv) a growing population and suburbanisation, particularly in Dublin, Cork and other coastal areas. Tourism has expanded rapidly, building on the country's "green image". This move towards a "new economy" has translated into a *decrease in the energy and material intensities of production* (per unit of GDP), but not an absolute decrease in environmental pressures. Overall, only a weak decoupling has taken place, compared to best international practices. Transition to the new economy has also translated into higher land prices and an *increase in environmental pressures relating to consumption*: greater waste generation, greater motorisation and mobility, greater land consumption, and related demands for environmental infrastructure.

Some *sectors and industries* that have serious negative impacts on the environment continue to benefit from low taxation and from subsidies, including EU support. For example, *peat based electricity production* is controversial given its low economic efficiency (as a subsidised activity) and environmental effects (air emissions, damage to landscapes and habitats); economic incentives with regard to *agriculture* should be reconsidered under the revised EU Common Agricultural Policy, to take advantage of "cross-compliance" opportunities (making farm support conditional on compliance with environmental standards) and agri-environmental payments (under the REPS programme).

In 1997, Ireland issued a national *Strategy for Sustainable Development* covering economic, social and environmental concerns. To implement this strategy, a high level inter-ministerial committee (the Environmental Network) and National Sustainable Development Partnership (Comhar) have been established. Comhar, which brings together a range of social partners, should help raise awareness, monitor progress and mobilise public support. Strategic environmental assessment has been introduced to systematically assess potential impacts of sectoral policies on the environment and sustainable development. They should be implemented in the context of the new National Development Plan 2000-06, marked by a significant phasing out of EU support.

Ireland has recognised a need to reform and strengthen its *spatial planning framework* at the national and regional level. The new Planning and Development Bill, when enacted and implemented, should introduce a more strategic and integrated approach to territorial development at the sub-national level. Strategic planning guidelines for the Dublin area have shown the way. A national spatial strategy should be prepared, providing a framework for longer-term spatial development at the national level. Systematic analysis of current and future pressures on Ireland's coastal zones, and of policy options to manage their future development and protection, needs to be carried out.

Local Agenda 21s have been initiated. The Environmental Partnership Fund, supporting participatory local co -operation projects, will help broaden the local movement for sustainable development and encourage the activities of NGOs.

It is *recommended* to:

- make the *national Sustainable Development Strategy* fully operational, particularly within the context of the National Development Plan 2000-06 and other sectoral policy initiatives;

- promote better integration of environmental concerns in sectoral policies, for example by using *environmental impact assessments* of plans, programmes and projects;

- reduce distortions created by subsidies for *energy and agricultural production*, and consider using cross-compliance mechanisms if support payments are granted;

- adopt and implement the new *planning and development bill*, providing a greater role for strategic guidelines and regional co-ordination on protection and development of urban and coastal areas;

- complete and implement the *national spatial strategy* to provide a framework for long-term spatial development at the national level;

- facilitate *participation and partnership* of local community groups and environmental NGOs in preparing, implementing and monitoring Local Agenda 21 initiatives, including through the Environmental Partnership Fund.

Towards sustainable transport

Since 1994, Ireland has successfully implemented a range of *regulatory measures* to reduce negative environmental externalities associated with transport. EU vehicle and fuel standards have been implemented effectively and on time. Leaded fuel was phased out from 1 January 2000. A national scrapping programme between 1995 and 1997 led to the removal of some 61 000 old vehicles (6% of the fleet at the time). Wide-ranging traffic management measures implemented in the Dublin region since 1997 (e.g. environmental traffic cells, parking management, dedicated bus corridors) have helped reduce congestion significantly. Economic instruments (taxes on vehicle sales, fuel and registration) are used to encourage the purchase of smaller and/or cleaner vehicles. Public transport passes provided to employees are given tax exempt status, and expenses associated with passenger car commuting are not deductible from income tax. EIA procedures, which are well-established in Ireland, are routinely applied in the case of large transport projects; public participation appears to be active and adequate.

Nevertheless, there is a need to expand *transport infrastructure*, particularly motorways, high-quality dual carriageways, public transport and links to ports and airports. This need has thus far been largely addressed through use of EU funds. Public-private partnerships are not widely utilised, and the User-Pays Principle is weakly implemented; their increased application should be considered, especially in view of increasing operational and maintenance expenditure and reduced EU support. Co-ordination of responses to increases in both international freight movement and passenger traffic has not yet been adequately addressed: the result is over-concentration of traffic in the Dublin area. Poor land use planning and the lack of integration of spatial planning with traffic management objectives, together with rising land prices and income levels, have encouraged urban sprawl and increasing personal mobility. The recently passed Strategic Planning Guidelines for the Dublin Area may help address this problem. Overall, there is not enough emphasis on taxing vehicle use, and possibly too much on vehicle ownership. Fuel prices are relatively low compared to those in neighbouring countries; apart from two bridges in Dublin, road tolls have not yet been used. Ireland's implementation of emissions testing for in-use vehicles, which has been delayed, should be given priority. *Looking ahead*, decisions made in the late 1990s will provide certain benefits, but the likely continuation of economic growth will generate further increases in freight traffic, urban sprawl and personal mobility. This will present major challenges regarding the environment and sustainable development.

It is *recommended* to:

– accelerate and expand application of *in-use vehicle emissions testing* (including for second-hand imports);

- continue to implement inter-modal *demand management measures* in Dublin and other major cities, in order to stimulate demand for public transport and limit demand for private vehicles (e.g. environmental traffic cells, parking management, dedicated bus corridors);

- accelerate completion of *congestion-alleviating road infrastructure* (e.g. bypasses, ring roads, tunnels);

- implement measures (e.g. planning, economic incentives) to *shift freight and passenger traffic* out of Dublin to the extent feasible;

- seek better application of the *User-Pays Principle* to road transport, giving special consideration to an increase in vehicle use taxation (e.g. fuel taxation) relative to ownership taxation (e.g. vehicle registration, sales tax), and to other economic instruments.

3. International Co-operation

Ireland, which is heavily dependent on both exports and imports of goods and services, is attracting foreign direct investment flows. It wants at the same time to retain its "green" image in order to promote agricultural exports and attract international tourism. Beginning its full-scale *international environmental co-operation* relatively recently, Ireland has ratified a very large number of significant international agreements on protection of the environment during the last 15 years while transposing very thoroughly nearly all EU directives. Irish environmental law has been driven to a large extent by that of Europe, and investment in environmental protection has mainly been funded by EU Structural and Cohesion Funds. Ireland is the cohesion country that has attracted the greatest amount of European support. At the same time, its economic development during the 1990s has been the most rapid in Europe: it is now the cohesion country with the highest GDP per capita and is a very active partner in the framework of the EU.

Ireland actively participates in *global environmental co-operation*, as well as North-east Atlantic and Pan-European co-operative activities. It has banned disposal of industrial waste and of sewage sludge at sea, together with incineration at sea. Progress has been made concerning surveillance of ships in the Irish Sea that transport hazardous goods or radioactive material. Prior notification of passage is taking place on an increasing basis. Ireland co-operates with Northern Ireland on many local issues, and further progress can be expected. Co-operation with the United Kingdom on protection of the marine environment has been thorough and fruitful. Ireland has contributed to the protection of biological diversity by designating a significant part of its territory for conservation, in the framework of EU directives or under the Ramsar Convention. It has also designated all of its marine waters as a whale sanctuary. Ireland has increased aid to developing countries since 1992 by the largest percentage of all DAC countries; its level of aid is now much higher than the DAC average.

Reflecting the lower priority given to *international issues* over many years, as well as its unexpectedly rapid economic growth, Ireland has had difficulty meeting agreed emissions targets. NO_x emissions have increased since 1994 instead of being stabilised at their 1987 level, as agreed under the Sofia Protocol. The national target for CO_2 emissions in 2000 will most likely be exceeded, as measures taken so far are inadequate. SO_2 emissions, which are significant in relative terms (compared with those in other western European countries), will require substantial reduction in 2000 to meet requirements of the Oslo Protocol. Ireland is the only EU country that did not sign the Protocol on VOCs. In addition, implementation of a number of EU directives is not fully consistent with EU deadlines (e.g. for drinking water quality in a number of small rural communities, and for a large number of Habitat sites). Progress towards developing Local Agenda 21s has been fairly slow. Concerning protection of the marine environment from land based sources of pollution, measures have been initiated but have had little effect so far. In the context of energy policy, exploitation of peat bogs of European significance has been subsidised and has led to the disruption of peat habitats and to large emissions of greenhouse gases per unit of electricity produced by peat-fuelled power stations.

Major difficulties probably lie ahead, due to progressive reduction of EU funding and the increasing operating costs and investment expenditure for new facilities. Challenges include meeting deadlines for completing waste water treatment plants, requirements for higher drinking water quality, and new international commitments concerning reduction of air emissions (Kyoto, Gothenburg). Stringent measures to control air emissions now need to be taken, having been postponed for a considerable time.

It is *recommended* to:

– strengthen co-operation with *Northern Ireland* on all relevant aspects of environmental protection and nature conservation in boundary regions and, where appropriate, on an all-island basis;

– promote activities at the local, national and international level aimed at protecting the *marine environment*, in particular from land based sources of pollution;

– ensure effective protection of designated *nature protection* areas under international or EU schemes by increasing resources for management and conservation, public consultation and awareness raising, and for compensating affected parties where necessary;

– give particular attention to *protecting peat bogs* of great ecological significance;

- adopt and strengthen measures to reduce *emissions of SO$_2$ and NO$_x$* with a view to meeting international commitments;
- take measures to reduce *VOCs emissions* with a view to conforming to international standards (EU legislation, Gothenburg);
- take measures to limit increases of *greenhouse gas emissions* to meet the Kyoto target, despite rapid economic growth;
- continue ongoing efforts to increase Irish *official development aid.*

1

THE CONTEXT

1. The Physical Context

The *Republic of Ireland* is bounded on the west and south by the Atlantic Ocean, and on the north by Northern Ireland (Figure 1.1). The Atlantic waters lying off the south coast are known as the Celtic Sea. To the east is the Irish Sea, which separates the island of Ireland from Great Britain. The Republic of Ireland has an area of 70 282 km². Its widest extensions are 486 kilometres north-south and 275 kilometres east-west.

Ireland is a *lowland country*. Several coastal mountain ranges surround the broad central calcareous plain, whose flatness is relieved in many places by low hills and ridges. The country's highest point is Carrantwohil (1 041 metres). Much of the 7 100 kilometre coastline is heavily indented, particularly along the entire western seaboard. The *climate* is temperate oceanic, influenced by a combination of the warm North Atlantic drift and prevailing winds from the south-west. It has a markedly maritime character; the range of mean temperatures over the year is relatively narrow, from 5 °C in winter to 15 °C in summer. Mean annual rainfall is 1 000 to 1 400 mm in the west and 750 to 1 000 mm in the east, while 2 000 mm is not uncommon in some mountain areas.

The Shannon, Ireland's longest river (370 kilometres), and several other rivers flow slowly through the central plain. The rivers on the seaward side of the mountain ranges are short and flow rapidly to the sea. Including approximately 6 000 lakes, *inland surface waters* cover 2% of the country's total area and provide rich fishery resources.

Ireland has one of the highest proportions of *land* devoted to agriculture in Europe (64%). Grassland, mainly grazed by beef and dairy herds (16 million head of cattle and sheep), covers 51% of total land area; arable and permanent crop land covers nearly 13%, and forest and other wooded land nearly 9%. There are extensive bogs in some parts of the country. Over the last three decades, the

Figure 1.1 **Map of Ireland**

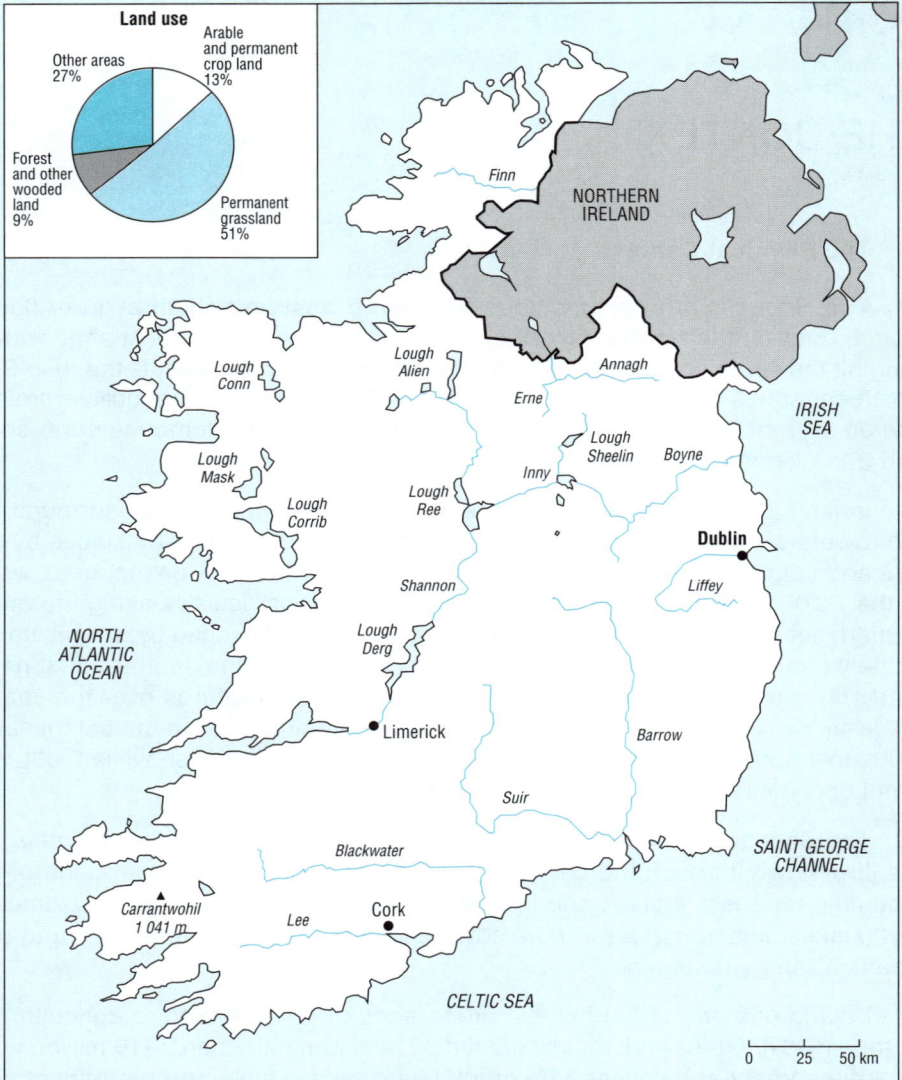

Land use
Arable and permanent crop land 13%
Other areas 27%
Forest and other wooded land 9%
Permanent grassland 51%

amount of cropland has remained stable; there has been a 22% decrease in permanent grassland and a 21% increase in forested area.

Ireland is not well endowed with *natural resources*. Since there are few indigenous sources of fuel, it is dependent on imports (mainly of oil and coal) to meet nearly 90% of primary energy requirements. Peat has been used as fuel for several centuries. The production life of bogs is some 30 years. Natural gas is exploited on the south coast (Kinsale Head), but this is expected to end by 2005.

2.   The Human Context

Ireland has a *population* of 3.7 million, of which one-third lives in Dublin and its surrounding seven counties (1.2 million) and in the counties of Cork (127 000) and Limerick (52 000). Average density (53 inhabitants per km^2) is relatively low. Outside Dublin and the eastern part of the country, the population is highly dispersed. Nearly everyone speaks English. There are around 80 000 native Irish speakers, largely in the western part of the country (Gaeltacht).

The 30% *population increase* over the last four decades followed a decline from 6.5 million in 1840 (26 counties) to 2.8 million in the early 1960s, mainly due to emigration following the Great Famine of the 1840s. Until 1970, *fall in rural population* resulted from both emigration and migration to urban areas. Since then, the urban population has continued to grow; the rate of increase slowed from 33 000 per year in the 1970s to 10 000 in the 1990s. Ireland is currently experiencing rapid *suburbanisation*, characterised by low-density residential, business and commercial development around towns and cities. Some 52% of the population lives within ten kilometres of the coast.

Ireland's *education and training* system is still maturing and continues to be upgraded and modernised. The educational level of the adult population is below the OECD average, for both upper secondary and university education. The ratio of students to teaching staff is above the OECD average.

The Irish *population is relatively young* (44% of the population is currently under 25) but is gradually ageing, as shown by an increase in the ageing index (over 65 years/under 15 years) from a third in 1960 to half in 1997. Substantial *health improvements* have been achieved in recent decades, with a considerable increase in life expectancy at birth. The development of sanitation infrastructure, leading to the elimination of many water-borne diseases, has been one of the main reasons for improved public health in this century. However, life expectancy at middle age remains lower than in most other EU countries.

In 1999, *unemployment* was around 6%, below the OECD and EU averages. Its rapid decrease, from 16% in 1993, is the result of robust economic growth, which has served not only to boost demand for labour but also to encourage a reversal of net migration flows, especially in the case of skilled workers. Services absorb 62% of the labour force, industry 29% and agriculture the remaining 9%.

3. The Economic Context

The Irish economy has notched up five years of *remarkable economic performance*. In 1999, *GDP* reached IEP 67 billion (USD 91 billion at current prices), following GDP growth averaging 9% a year in 1994-99 (Figure 1.2). High GDP growth rates are expected to continue for a while (a first estimate is 7.5% for 2000). GDP per capita has reached USD 20 600 (expressed in purchasing power parities), higher than the EU average (Annex II). Government debt in relation to GDP has shrunk by nearly half and is well below the Maastricht threshold of 60%. Inflation remained at around 2% until the end of 1999, despite the economic boom.

There is no single explanation for the changes in economic performance: first around 1987, when deterioration ceased and performance began to improve, and then around 1994, when the boom began. Partnership agreements between trade unions, business and employer organisations have ensured strong *social consensus*, reflected in particular by the moderate increase in private sector wages. Membership in the *European Union* has also been of great benefit: the net inflow of EU (including Common Agricultural Policy) funds reached 4.2% of GDP in 1997 (down to about 2% of GDP in 1999), and the Single Market is more favourable to the peripheral countries, including Ireland, than to most of the other Member States. A massive inflow of *foreign direct investment* has been encouraged, in part, by a low corporate tax rate of 10% in the manufacturing and international financial services sectors. Ireland's share of OECD total FDI inflows surged in the 1990s, reaching a level out of proportion to its share of GDP; in 1997, it ranked fifth in the world as a destination of direct investment outflows from the United States.

Over the last decade, the share of *industry* in GDP has increased and now accounts for 39%. Industrial development has mainly been in the form of export-platform manufacturing (Ireland is an attractive base from which to supply the EU market), particularly of computers, semiconductors, office equipment, software, pharmaceuticals, electrical engineering and soft drinks. The share of *services* has remained high, at around 56% of GDP. Over two-thirds of service firms are in the financial sector, especially following the creation of the International Financial Services Centre (IFSC) in Dublin in 1993. In the 1990s, the number of overseas visitors doubled (from 3 million in 1990 to 6 million in 1998).

Agriculture's share of GDP has fallen from 9 to 5% over the last decade. Agriculture still accounts for 9% of total employment, which is high by EU standards. Accession to the then EEC in 1973 gave Ireland access to guaranteed markets and prices under the Common Agricultural Policy (CAP), leading to substantial growth in output. The traditionally mixed character of Irish farming has

Figure 1.2 **Economic structure and trends**

GDP[a] in Ireland, 1980-99

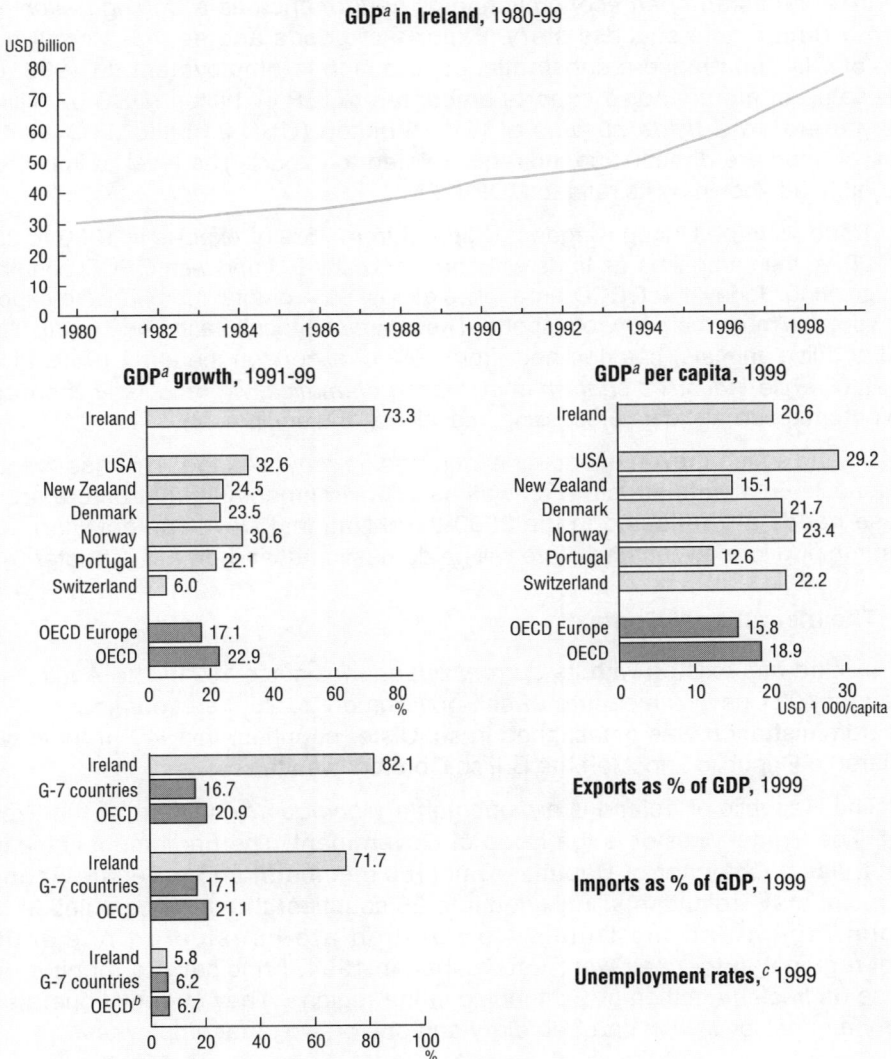

USD billion

GDP[a] growth, 1991-99

Ireland	73.3
USA	32.6
New Zealand	24.5
Denmark	23.5
Norway	30.6
Portugal	22.1
Switzerland	6.0
OECD Europe	17.1
OECD	22.9

0   20   40   60   80
%

GDP[a] per capita, 1999

Ireland	20.6
USA	29.2
New Zealand	15.1
Denmark	21.7
Norway	23.4
Portugal	12.6
Switzerland	22.2
OECD Europe	15.8
OECD	18.9

0   10   20   30
USD 1 000/capita

Ireland	82.1
G-7 countries	16.7
OECD	20.9

Exports as % of GDP, 1999

Ireland	71.7
G-7 countries	17.1
OECD	21.1

Imports as % of GDP, 1999

Ireland	5.8
G-7 countries	6.2
OECD[b]	6.7

0   20   40   60   80   100
%

Unemployment rates,[c] 1999

a) GDP at 1991 price levels and purchasing power parities.
b) Includes Secretariat estimates.
c) Per cent of total labour force.
Source: OECD.

given way to specialisation and increased mechanisation. There has been a significant decrease in tillage area, with approximately balancing increases in the amount of land used for pasture and silage.

Ireland has an *open economy*, and its performance as a *trading nation* has been a remarkable success story. Exports of goods and services contribute 82% of GDP and make a substantial contribution to employment. In 1998, the total value of merchandise exports amounted to IEP 44 billion (USD 62 billion) and generated a *trade surplus* of IEP 15 billion (USD 21 billion). Over half a million jobs are directly and indirectly related to export. The level of imports is also high, as shown by its ratio to GDP (72%).

Trade with the United Kingdom dropped from 75% of exports in 1960 to 22% in 1998, at the same time as trade with the rest of the EU and with OECD countries was growing. Today, the OECD area takes almost 90% of total merchandise exports and supplies more than 80% of imports. The share of agriculture in trade (particularly food and live animals) has declined (from 60% of exports in the early 1960s to 9% in 1998), while *industry's share has increased dramatically* (particularly chemicals and pharmaceuticals, data processing, machinery and equipment).

Ireland's high growth economy is *undergoing rapid change*. This has created bottlenecks in all infrastructure as well as in environmental infrastructure areas. These needs are reflected in the 2000-2006 National Development Plan, and most funding for new infrastructure will be domestic rather than EU (Chapter 5).

4. The Institutional Context

Ireland has existed with its *current boundaries* since 1921. The Anglo-Irish Treaty of 1921 gave a measure of self-government to 26 Irish counties; a separate administration was established in six Ulster counties. In 1949, Ireland was declared a Republic and it left the British Commonwealth.

The Republic of Ireland is a *parliamentary democracy* headed by the President. The Prime Minister is the Head of Government. The Parliament is bicameral: it has a Chamber of Deputies-Dail (166 members) and a Senate-Seanad (60 members). Ireland is still divided into 26 counties; the three counties in the Dublin region and the Dublin Corporation are considered one entity. Eight regional authorities were established in 1994, principally to monitor and advise on implementation of EU funding in the regions. They currently operate at a very modest level, with one Secretary and one or two other employees.

Central environmental administration

The *Department of the Environment and Local Government* (DOELG) has *wide-ranging responsibilities* relating to nine main sectors: local government;

environment; water services; road transportation and safety; housing; planning and urban renewal; the construction industry; the electoral system; and protective and amenity services (such as fire services, emergency planning, libraries and the arts) (Figure 1.3). DOELG's mission is to ensure, in partnership with a strengthened system of local government, that Ireland has a high quality environment where infrastructure and amenities meet economic, social and environmental needs and development is properly planned and sustainable. In the area of environmental protection (including air, water and waste management, but excluding nature protection) it defines policies and strategies, prepares legislation and develops guidelines for local authorities. Overall, DOELG has a staff of about 830, including 200 located in Ballina and Shannon.

Given its wide-ranging responsibilities and the very low share (2%) of revenues from local taxation in the Irish fiscal system (Table 1.1), *DOELG annual expenditure* is around 1% of GDP. Over 90% of its expenditure goes *via* local authorities to support public investment relating, for instance, to roads, water supply, sewerage and waste water treatment, housing and urban renewal. Most of these activities have been major beneficiaries of EU co-financing.

Various bodies operate under the aegis of DOELG. It is complemented by the *Environmental Protection Agency* (EPA), an independent statutory body established in 1992 to control and regulate activities likely to pose major risks to environmental quality; undertake general monitoring of the environment; provide support, back-up and advisory services to public authorities; and promote and co-ordinate environmental research. The EPA carries out integrated pollution control

Table 1.1 **Fiscal revenues,** 1997

(%)

	Supranational	Federal or central	State	Local	Social security funds	Total
Ireland	1.1	85.2	–	2.1	11.5	100
United States	–	44.1	19.3	12.3	24.2	100
New Zealand	–	94.6	–	5.4	–	100
Denmark	0.5	65.2	–	31.2	3.2	100
Norway	–	60.5	–	18.3	21.2	100
Portugal	0.6	66.6	–	5.7	27.1	100
Switzerland	–	27.9	19.9	15.3	36.9	100

Source: OECD.

Figure 1.3   **Organisational chart of the Department of the Environment and Local Government**[a]

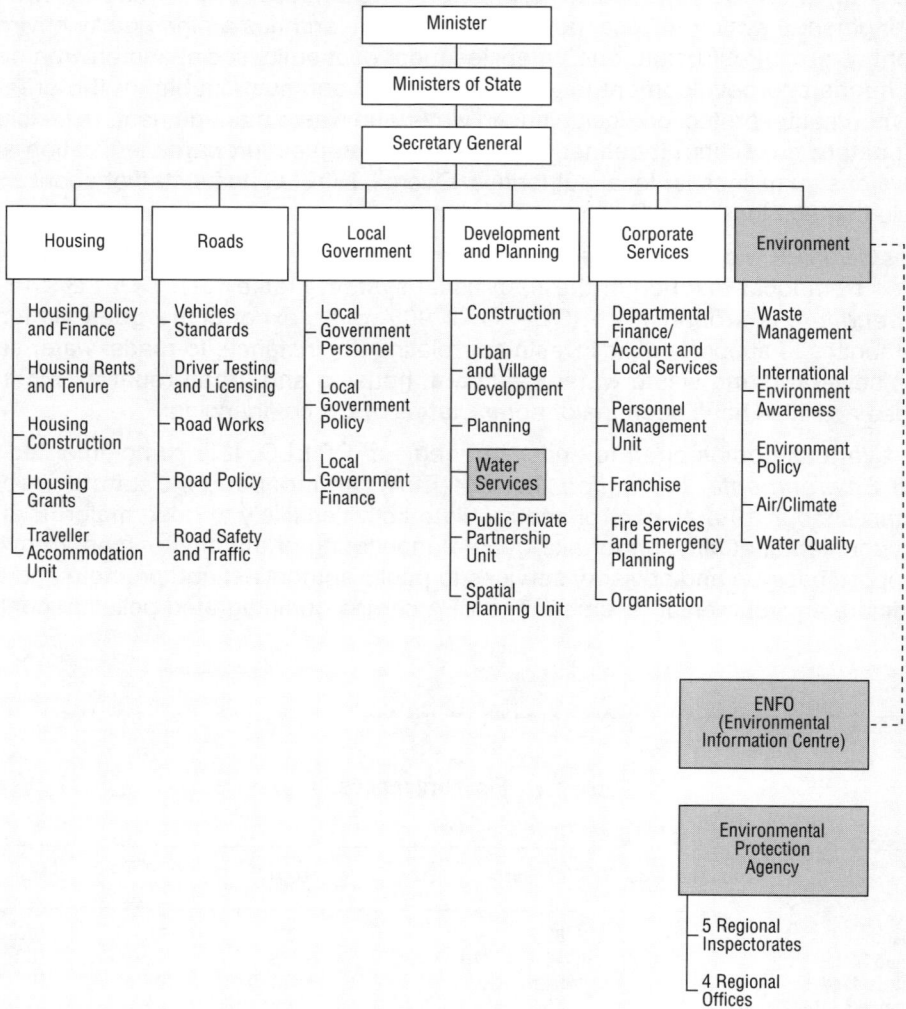

a) Nature conservation is the responsibility of the Department of Arts, Heritage, Gaeltacht and the Islands (DAHGI).
Source: DOELG.

(IPC) licensing of scheduled industrial enterprises, as well as licensing all significant waste disposal and recovery operations and permitting large-scale petrol storage facilities. It has a staff of 189 and an annual budget of IEP 12.3 million; there are five regional inspectorates and four regional offices. *ENFO*, an environmental information centre operated by DOELG since 1990, provides free-of-charge information to users ranging from primary schools to specialised researchers. ENFO has a staff of 11 and an annual budget of IEP 1 million.

In 1992, DOELG entered into an agreement with the *Economic and Social Research Institute (ESRI)* to develop research into economic aspects of environmental policy, with particular reference to pricing and economic instruments. The *An Board Pleanála* (Irish Planning Appeals Board), an independent statutory body established in 1976, deals with appeals, references and other matters relating to legislation on land use planning, water pollution, air pollution and building control. It has ten Board members, and an authorised staff of 110, and is financed through transfers from the central budget as well as some income from planning appeal fees.

The *Department of Arts, Heritage, Gaeltacht and the Islands (DAHGI)* has the main role in addressing *nature protection* issues. DAHGI sets and implements policy and legislation for the conservation and management of Ireland's heritage, including its natural heritage. The *Heritage Council*, established in 1995, defines priorities and recommends policies to protect and increase awareness of the country's heritage in the areas of wildlife, archaeology, architecture and inland waterways. It is an independent State body with a staff of 12 and annual funding of IEP 4 million, channelled through DAHGI. The *National Parks and Wildlife Service* of DAHGI has a staff of 250 employees (mostly field management staff) and an annual budget of IEP 25 million.

Although DOELG has the main environmental policy-making role, *other administrative bodies* besides DAHGI are directly responsible for ensuring that environmental effects of their respective policies, programmes and projects are fully considered before decisions are taken. An *Environmental Network of Government Departments* was created in 1994 to promote better information exchange on issues of environmental importance, and to support the work of environment units established in the main economic departments. Since 1995, a *Joint Parliamentary Committee on Environment and Local Government* monitors implementation of national strategies relating to the environment. An interdepartmental steering group on sustainable development indicators was created in 1998. The *National Sustainable Development Partnership* (Comhar) was established in 1999 to encourage greater public participation in environmental policy formulation. Comhar is a forum for national consultation and dialogue between the State, economic sectors, NGOs and academics.

Environmental responsibilities of local authorities

The *34 county authorities* (29 County Councils and five urban authorities: the Dublin, Cork, Galway, Limerick and Waterford County Boroughs) implement national environmental policies under the co-ordination and supervision of DOELG. Some *54 borough and urban councils* (five Borough Corporations and 49 Urban District Councils) operate as authorities for physical planning, litter control and, in some cases, licensing of discharges to sewers. There are about 30 000 employees in these *88 Local Councils*, of whom about 4 000 are engaged part or full time in providing environmental services. The city and county local authorities (including all urban authorities within the counties) are managed by city and county managers (senior local public servants). Local authorities depend upon funds received from or through DOELG to finance much of their environmental activity.

Since 1992, the EPA has had a monitoring and oversight role in relation to local authorities' performance of their *statutory environmental protection functions*. Local authority functions include:

- provision of drinking water, waste water collection and treatment, solid waste management, and litter prevention and control;
- implementation of legislation on air/water pollution and waste management for activities other than those controlled and regulated by the EPA; and
- promoting public awareness of environmental issues.

Local government legislation also gives local authorities discretion in providing a wide range of amenities and recreational facilities. Local authorities are expected to take full account of environmental concerns in exercising infrastructure-related responsibilities.

Local authorities are required to prepare *development plans*, to be reviewed every five years including through comprehensive public consultation procedures. These plans provide the framework for more detailed land use planning, and for granting or refusing permission for proposed developments. Local authorities must also adopt *management plans* relating to pollution abatement and control in order to provide an overall framework for air quality, water quality and waste management. There are general waste management plans for all local authorities, but only a few air quality management plans; water quality management plans have mainly been prepared jointly by a number of local authorities and on a catchment basis.

Funding of *capital investment* is almost entirely covered by the central budget. Local taxation only relates to industrial and commercial properties and does not apply to household property. Most major water services schemes are co-financed by the EU Cohesion Fund, administered by central government authorities on a project basis. Somewhat greater discretion and responsibility are assigned to local authorities for small water and sewerage schemes. Municipal waste services, predominantly the responsibility of local authorities, are increasingly provided by the private sector. The creation of a Local Government Fund in 1999 has placed significant additional resources (IEP 590 million in 1999) at the disposal of local authorities for *current expenditure*. DOELG also operates an *Environmental Partnership Fund* to provide 50% support to environmental awareness projects in the context of Local Agenda 21.

5. Environmental Legislation

Environmental legislation includes various Acts, accompanied by Regulations (Table 1.2). To a large extent this legislation has been influenced by *EU legislation*.

Physical planning, which is subject to long established legislation, is one of the main instruments of environmental protection. The 1963 Local Government (Planning and Development) Act provided the framework for planning and development of urban areas. The 1990 Local Government (Planning and Development) Regulations set out in detail the procedures required for conducting environmental impact assessments. The *Planning and Development Bill* planned to be adopted in 2000 will replace, update and consolidate the Local Government (Planning and Development) Acts.

In the area of *pollution prevention and control*, the 1977 Local Government (Water Pollution) Act includes provisions concerning licensing of discharges to waters and sewers, water quality standards, water quality management plans, civil liability of polluters and by-laws regulating agricultural activities. The 1987 Air Pollution Act provides a comprehensive statutory framework for controlling air quality. Radical changes to waste management practice were introduced with the 1996 Waste Management Act, which sets out the responsibilities and functions of individuals, and of local and central authorities, relating to waste. The 1992 Environmental Protection Agency Act defines responsibilities for issuing EPA pollution control licenses. The 1990 Derelict Sites Act places a duty on all owners and occupiers (including of dwellings) to ensure that properties are not, and do not become, derelict. Many pollution prevention and control regulations have been issued under the 1972 European Communities Act.

In the area of *nature conservation*, under the 1963 Local Government (Planning and Development) Act, development is to be controlled in areas of outstanding natural beauty and amenity, areas of scenic importance, views and prospects, and other areas of amenity value. Protection of wild fauna and flora, and conservation of areas with specific wildlife values, are governed by the 1976 Wildlife Act. A 1999 Amendment Bill to this Act aims at providing legal protection to a network of ecologically important sites (Natural Heritage Areas), as well as improving or introducing a variety of other wildlife conservation measures. Regulations issued in 1997 provide for the designation and protection of Special Areas of Conservation (SACs). The 1933 Forestry Act contains restrictions on tree harvesting outside urban areas. The 1933 Foreshore Act gives the Marine and Natural Resources Minister power to control activities, within a 12-mile limit, which may impact adversely on flora and fauna, amenities or public rights of way on the seashore.

Table 1.2 **Selected legislation relating to the environment**

1933	Forestry Act (amended in 1946 and 1988)
1933	Foreshore Act (amended in 1992 and 1998)
1963	Local Government (Planning and Development) Act (amended several times)
1968	Continental Shelf Act
1972	European Communities Act
1976	Wildlife Act (Amendment Bill in 1999)
1977	Local Government (Water Pollution) Act (amended in 1990)
1982	Litter Act
1983	Local Government (Financial Provisions) Act (amended in 1997)
1986	Urban Renewal Act
1987	Air Pollution Act
1988	Oil Pollution of the Sea (Civil Liability and Compensation) Act (amended in 1998)
1990	Derelict Sites Act
1991	Sea Pollution Act (amended in 1999)
1991	Radiological Protection Act
1992	Environmental Protection Agency Act
1996	Waste Management Act
1996	Dumping at Sea Act
1997	Litter Pollution Act
1998	Fisheries and Foreshore (Amendment) Act
2000	Planning and Development Bill
2000	Local Government Bill

Source: DOELG.

Part I

POLLUTION PREVENTION
AND CONTROL

2

WATER MANAGEMENT

1. Current Situation and Trends

Freshwater resources

Ireland has *abundant water resources* (12 000 m³/capita annually), with plentiful rainfall evenly distributed throughout the year. Water bodies, which cover 2% of its surface, are among the most prominent features of the Irish landscape. Part of the country is *prone to flooding*, due to the very low gradient of its rivers. Mean annual precipitation is 1 150 mm, of which 540 mm is lost to evapotranspiration (Figure 2.1). Most renewable freshwater resources consist of surface water (42 billion cubic metres); the rest (4 billion cubic metres) is groundwater.

Ireland has *some 400 river catchments*, mostly small and coastal. Surface water systems can be divided into two broad types: steep shingle streams flowing to the sea from coastal mountain ranges, and slow-flowing rivers and lake systems on the central plain, which also has extensive wetland areas. Irish rivers are relatively short. The longest is the Shannon (370 kilometres), followed by the Blackwater and Barrow. There are approximately *6 000 lakes*, mostly small; 24 have a surface area greater than 750 hectares. Lough Corrib (16 900 hectares) is the largest lake.

Almost a quarter of the population relies on *groundwater* for drinking water supply. Aquifers tend to be shallow and bores are less than 120 metres. There are deeper aquifers, but the water is thought to have a high mineral content and they have not been investigated in detail.

Water quality

The ecological condition of *rivers and streams* is assessed using a four-level scale. The assessment system includes consideration of physico-chemical parameters (including BOD, DO and nutrients), macro-invertebrates, plants, algae

Figure 2.1   **Water resources**[a]

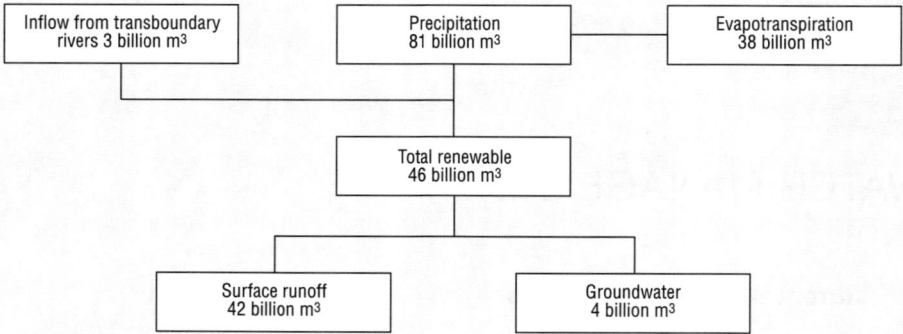

```
┌─────────────────────────┐   ┌─────────────────────────┐   ┌─────────────────────────┐
│ Inflow from transboundary│   │     Precipitation        │   │   Evapotranspiration     │
│   rivers 3 billion m³    │   │     81 billion m³        │   │     38 billion m³        │
└─────────────────────────┘   └─────────────────────────┘   └─────────────────────────┘
                    ┌─────────────────────────┐
                    │     Total renewable      │
                    │      46 billion m³       │
                    └─────────────────────────┘
        ┌─────────────────────────┐       ┌─────────────────────────┐
        │     Surface runoff       │       │      Groundwater         │
        │      42 billion m³       │       │      4 billion m³        │
        └─────────────────────────┘       └─────────────────────────┘
```

a) Average over several years.
Source: OECD.

Figure 2.2   **Water use,** late 1990s

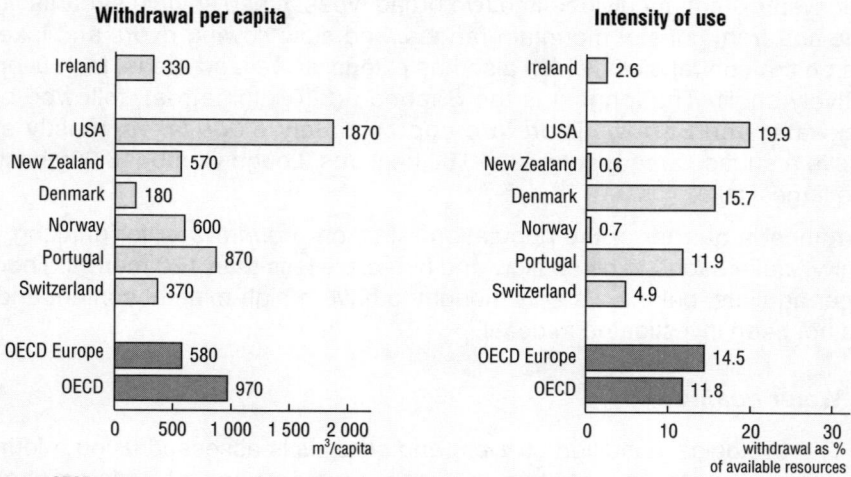

Withdrawal per capita

Ireland   330
USA   1870
New Zealand   570
Denmark   180
Norway   600
Portugal   870
Switzerland   370

OECD Europe   580
OECD   970

0   500 1 000 1 500 2 000
m³/capita

Intensity of use

Ireland   2.6
USA   19.9
New Zealand   0.6
Denmark   15.7
Norway   0.7
Portugal   11.9
Switzerland   4.9

OECD Europe   14.5
OECD   11.8

0   10   20   30
withdrawal as %
of available resources

Source: OECD.

and sewage fungus. The majority (67%) of monitored Irish rivers and streams are unpolluted, 18% are slightly polluted and 14% are moderately polluted; only 1% (122 kilometres) are seriously polluted. A database of nearly 3 000 kilometres of streams monitored since the early 1970s shows a substantial *decline in river water quality*. Over the last 30 years, the length of unpolluted rivers has fallen from 85 to 67% of the total.

Lakes are classified as oligotrophic/mesotrophic (satisfactory conditions) or eutrophic/hypertrophic (unsatisfactory conditions). The majority of monitored lakes (65% by surface area) are oligotrophic/mesotrophic; about 32% of surface area is eutrophic and 3% is hypertrophic. Bacteriological water quality is moni-tored at nine lake bathing sites. All these sites comply with mandatory EU values, and eight comply with more stringent guideline values. There has been an *improvement in lake water quality*, especially in some of the larger lakes. The pro-portion of strongly eutrophic lakes fell from 16 to 3% over ten years.

Nitrate levels in *groundwater* are generally below the 50mg/litre value for safe drinking water, and in the majority of cases are below 25mg/litre. *Faecal contami-nation* is widespread, with 34% of samples containing faecal coliforms.

Drinking water quality in *public water supplies* is reasonable, with 91% of samples complying with the EU's 1980 Drinking Water Directive. In 1991, 73% of households were connected to public water supply, 13% to private individual sup-ply, 8% to group schemes with public funding and 5% to group schemes with pri-vate funding. The quality of piped water from *group water supplies* (mostly privately owned and maintained, and mostly in rural areas) is variable. Around 200 000 people receive water of variable quality (based on coliform presence); overall, 400 000 people, whether or not they are served by group supplies, may receive water whose quality is substandard.

The quality of *marine bathing water* is good: 98% of the 121 monitored sites comply with mandatory EU requirements and about 80% comply with more strin-gent guideline values. The Cork and Broadmeadow *estuaries* show persistent signs of eutrophication, four estuaries show regular signs and five show occa-sional signs. Water quality for *shellfish gathering* in marine and estuarine areas is assessed using a three-level scale. Of the 58 sites monitored, 32 are "A" quality (can be eaten without treatment), 17 are "B"(must be purified for 48 hours) and nine are "C" (must be purified for more than two months before public consumption).

Pressures on water resources

Pressures on water quantities

With abundant and well-distributed rainfall, low population density and little irrigation, *overall pressure on water resources through withdrawal is low*. Intensity of water use at less than 3%, and consumption at 330 cubic metres per capita, are both well below the OECD average (Figure 2.2). Total annual water withdrawal has increased slowly. Freshwater withdrawals are mainly for public water supply (40%), electrical cooling (24%), other industrial uses (21%) and agricultural uses (15%). Groundwater resources are not heavily exploited.

Pressures on water quality

Over the last 30 years, the total length of moderately or slightly polluted *rivers* has increased from 9 to 32%. Water pollution is now mainly due to nutrient contamination from agricultural sources (crop and livestock production). However, the proportion of seriously polluted rivers and streams has fallen from 6 to 1%, thanks to efforts to abate point source pollution from municipalities and industries. Over the last ten years, better *lake* water quality has resulted from improvements in sewage treatment facilities, particularly the introduction of nutrient removal processes.

Some beaches in rural areas fail to meet mandatory EU requirements for *marine bathing water* owing to diffuse sources of runoff, mainly related to farming. The quality of beaches in urban areas should improve with ongoing investments in waste water treatment infrastructure. Some Irish *estuaries* are at risk from eutrophication because of their low flushing rates and high nutrient inputs from agricultural and, in some cases, urban sources.

Sewage discharges account for a significant share of river and stream pollution (Table 2.1). The catchments most sensitive to water pollution contain the

Table 2.1 **Main sources of pollution of rivers and streams,** 1997
(% of monitoring points)

	Serious pollution[a]	Moderate pollution[a]	Slight pollution[a]
Sewage	48	25	24
Agriculture	25	46	47
Industry	21	11	9
Other/unknown	6	18	20
Total	100	100	100

a) Refers to four-level classification scale, mainly reflecting the effects of organic wastes on water quality (deoxygenation and eutrophication). Unpolluted rivers also constitute a class.
Source: EPA.

lakes Loughs Ree, Derg, Oughter and Leane, and the rivers Boyne, Castelbar, Nenagh, Camlin, Liffey and Tullamore. However, *total pollution loads from point sources are declining* following a substantial investment programme in sewage treatment.

Pollution from agriculture has increased substantially over the last 30 years as a consequence of intensified *crop production* and *livestock raising*. Over a period of ten years, the national nitrogen balance (at soil surface) increased from 60 to 74 kg N/hectare of farmland. Application rates of both phosphate and nitrogenous fertilisers are high, well above the OECD average (Figure 2.3). Total consumption of commercial fertilisers (NPK) increased by 25% from 1980 to 1995, but has declined by 10% since then. Half the nutrients come from livestock manure, mostly that of cattle. Slurry spreading at inappropriate times, which occurs in many areas, is thought to contribute substantially to elevated nutrient levels in surface water, as well as runoff and spillage from storage tanks. Livestock density is far above the OECD and OECD Europe averages (Figure 2.4). Herd size has increased over the last 15 years by 11% for cattle, 78% for sheep and 78% for pigs. Intensity of *pesticide* use is about 2.5 kg active ingredients per hectare of crop land, in line with the OECD Europe average.

2. Responses

Legal and institutional framework

Public water supply is regulated by the 1878 Public Health Act, 1942 Water Supplies Act and 1964 Sanitary Service Act, which established the conditions under which local authorities should construct and operate drinking water utilities. Water quality started to be an issue at the national level in the 1970s, leading to enactment of the *1977 Local Government (Water Pollution) Act*. Water pollutants are defined very broadly, as they include effluents from all activities including mining. Since the early 1970s, EU Directives relating to water protection have been regularly incorporated in Irish legislation through Regulations. Nutrient management planning is covered by the 1977 Local Government (Water Pollution) Act as amended by the 1996 Waste Management Act. Regulations were issued on phosphorus in 1998 and groundwater protection in 1999.

Although the *Department of the Environment and Local Government* (DOELG) is responsible for formulating policy, programmes and legislation on water quality and supply services and on waste water-related services, a number of *other departments* have water management responsibilities. DOELG designates watercourses suitable for *salmon* according to the 1978 EU directive on the quality of fresh waters needing protection or improvement in order to support fish life. The Regional Fisheries Board, under the Marine and Natural Resources

Figure 2.3 **Agricultural inputs,** 1997

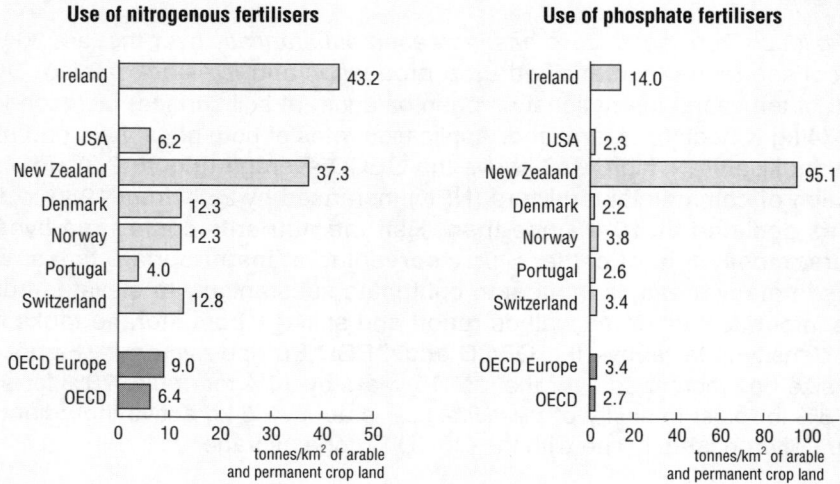

Use of nitrogenous fertilisers

Ireland 43.2
USA 6.2
New Zealand 37.3
Denmark 12.3
Norway 12.3
Portugal 4.0
Switzerland 12.8

OECD Europe 9.0
OECD 6.4

0 10 20 30 40 50
tonnes/km^2 of arable
and permanent crop land

Use of phosphate fertilisers

Ireland 14.0
USA 2.3
New Zealand 95.1
Denmark 2.2
Norway 3.8
Portugal 2.6
Switzerland 3.4

OECD Europe 3.4
OECD 2.7

0 20 40 60 80 100
tonnes/km^2 of arable
and permanent crop land

Source: FAO; OECD.

Figure 2.4 **Livestock^a density,** 1999

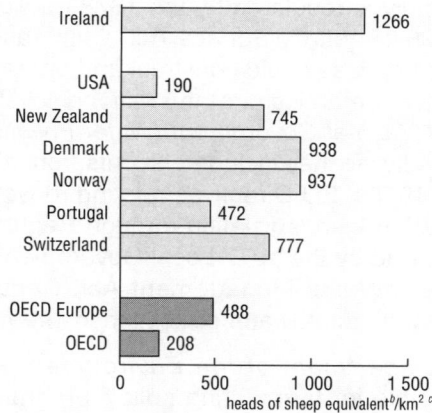

Ireland 1266
USA 190
New Zealand 745
Denmark 938
Norway 937
Portugal 472
Switzerland 777

OECD Europe 488
OECD 208

0 500 1 000 1 500
heads of sheep equivalent^b/km^2 ^{c}

a) Cattle, horses, pigs, hens, sheep and goats.
b) Based on equivalent coefficients in terms of manure:
    1 horse = 4.8 sheep; 1 pig = 1 goat = 1 sheep; 1 hen = 0.1 sheep; 1 cattle = 6 sheep.
c) Of arable, permanent crop land and permanent grassland.
Source: FAO; OECD.

Department, can undertake prosecutions for water pollution offences as part of its *coastal and inland fisheries* management function. The Department of Agriculture and Food administers agri-environmental schemes, including *measures to protect water from nutrient runoff.* The Office of Public Works, under the Finance Department, carries out *land drainage and flood protection* works according to the 1925 Drainage Act (amended 1945 and 1995). The Department of Public Enterprise carries out *geological surveys* that include groundwater resources.

The 34 *county and city authorities* have overall statutory responsibility for water management. This includes preparing and implementing catchment management plans and monitoring the state of water quality. DOELG can direct local authorities to prepare such catchment plans. The EPA is assisting with model terms of reference for the development of more comprehensive water management strategies. Local authorities also have flood management functions *in situ*ations where drainage districts have not been taken over by the Office of Public Works. Drinking water supply and sewage collection and treatment facilities are operated by the 54 *urban districts*, with some intercommunal grouping as in Dublin. In some cases, particularly in rural areas, water services are provided by local community initiatives. These "Group Water Schemes" are privately run; since 1997, the County Councils supervise their activities. There are about 1 000 public drinking water supply networks, of which many are small rural ones.

Objectives

A range of objectives derive from implementation of EU directives on water quality (surface water quality, water pollution control, groundwater quality, drinking water quality, urban waste water treatment, nitrates). For *fresh water and estuaries*, implementation of the 1991 Urban Waste water Treatment Directive implies upgrading sewage treatment plants with:

- phosphorus reduction facilities in sensitive catchments, by 1998;
- secondary treatment in cities with over 15 000 population equivalent, by 2001;
- secondary treatment in cities with 2 000-15 000 population equivalent, by 2006.

For *marine waters*, the objectives are less stringent:

- secondary treatment must be installed on plants serving 10 000-15 000 population equivalent, by 2006;
- appropriate treatment only (i.e. primary treatment may be sufficient) is required for smaller settlements, by 2006.

The 1997 *National Catchment-based Strategy against Eutrophication* sets objectives for river and lake conditions intended to protect fish species such as salmon and trout. The overall long-term goal for rivers is to achieve unpolluted status; for lakes, the aim is to achieve mesotrophic status for polluted ones and maintain the condition of oligotrophic lakes. The following interim targets are to be met by 2007:

- elimination of seriously polluted river stretches;
- improvement of river stretches slightly or moderately polluted;
- restoration of eutrophic lakes to satisfactory conditions, and improvement of hypertrophic lakes.

Regulatory instruments

Discharge permits

Since its inception in 1993, the Environmental Protection Agency (EPA) has implemented *Integrated Pollution Control* (i.e. single licensing for air emissions, waste water discharges, waste and noise generation) for larger industrial sites and large intensive pig and poultry production units. *County Councils*, which license point sources other than those addressed by the EPA, can attach specific pollution control conditions in licensing effluent discharges to waters or sewers from industry. They can also issue notices to control activities, such as farming, deemed to cause water pollution (specifying measures to be taken within a pre-scribed period to prevent water pollution) or require cessation of an activity causing water pollution. More than 1 300 such notices are issued annually; 90% concern the agricultural sector.

If a *breach of license* occurs, the licensing authority can take the person or agency responsible to court. Most EPA court actions are through the District Court. Fines are very low, but courts may require mitigation or remedying of any environmental damage caused by pollution. Indictable offences in the higher courts carry penalties of up to IEP 10 million on conviction. Adverse publicity following a court appearance has proved a powerful incentive for companies not to violate their licensing conditions.

Strategic and management plans

Catchment management plans are key non-statutory water planning documents. They establish specific goals for water quality and provide a framework for co-ordinating the actions of various agencies and groups involved in water management. To date, 15 catchment management plans have been adopted and ten are being prepared, covering 54% of total land area. Some plans have already been implemented, such as in the Lough Derg and Lough Ree catchments on the river Shannon and in three other large river catchments (the Suir,

Liffey and Boyne). Protection of surface waters used for abstraction of drinking water has a high priority under these plans. It has recently been decided to include groundwater and coastal water in the catchment plans and to extend the programme to all the catchments in Ireland.

A package of measures was put in place in 1998 to assist County Councils to manage the Group Water Schemes. Each Council must develop a *strategic rural water plan* identifying synergies in the development and operation of public and group schemes. A national overview committee and local management committees should be established, to ensure co-ordination and co-operation among the main agencies and groups involved in rural water services.

Under the Waste Management Act, County Councils may require farmers to develop *statutory nutrient management plans*. Under the Local Government (Water Pollution) Act, they can issue by-laws regulating certain agricultural activities. These plans and by-laws may include mandatory provisions covering effluent storage facilities and fertiliser and slurry application rates. Work has begun on nutrient management plans in the Lough Ree and Derg catchments, covering 10 600 km^2. *Standards for phosphorus* in surface waters are prescribed in the Water Pollution Act. Some County Councils have prepared draft by-laws to implement the 1998 phosphorus Regulations.

In 1999, guidelines were issued to local authorities for development and implementation of *sludge management plans*. It is estimated that between 1993 and 2013, the volume of sludge from waste water treatment plants will increase more than three-fold (from 38 000 to 130 000 tonnes dry solids).

Flood control includes maintenance by the Office of Public Works of 12 000 kilometres of river and stream channel and 700 kilometres of embankments. There are plans to address urban flood control, for example around Gort in the County Galway.

Monitoring

Ireland has a well-developed monitoring system for water quality in *rivers, lakes, groundwater and marine bathing water*. Specific monitoring programmes are in place in 23 *estuaries*, focusing on eutrophication. Sampling for toxic contaminants is limited, reflecting the low level of heavy industry. Monitoring of *shellfish areas* covers both commercial and recreational gathering.

Economic instruments

Concerning *households*, Ireland presently *does not use water pricing* for public water supply and sanitation (Table 2.2). "Domestic rates" (i.e. local property taxes applying to households) were abolished in 1978, and with them the contribution made by households to the cost of water services in urban areas; County Councils in rural areas retained their long-standing power to charge for domestic water supply. In 1983, local authority powers to charge for services were extended, including a new power to charge for water in urban areas, with the local authorities having discretion as to services to be charged for and the amount of the charges. By 1996, water supply charges (with flat fees) had been developed in 86 of the 88 Local Councils (all except Dublin and Limerick); 31 had also levied waste water charges. In 1997, a decision was taken to discontinue separate

Table 2.2 **Water prices,** 1998

(USD/m³)

	At current exchange rates	At current PPPs
Ireland[a]		
Dublin	0	0
Cork	0	0
USA		
New York	0.43	0.43
Los Angeles	0.58	0.58
Miami	0.36	0.36
New Zealand		
Wellington	0.63	0.82
Auckland	0.46	0.59
Denmark		
Copenhagen	1.68	1.34
Aarhus	1.26	1.00
Norway		
Oslo[b]	0.47	0.39
Bergen[b]	1.30	1.09
Portugal		
Lisbon	0.97	1.39
Porto	1.02	1.46
Switzerland		
Geneva	2.14	1.54
Zurich	1.88	1.35

Notes: Prices of water supply for a family of four (two adults and two children) living in a house with a garden, with annual consumption of 200 m³. VAT not included.

a) Ireland does not use water pricing for public water supply and sanitation.

b) Unmeasured data: refer to the average price.

Source: IWSA.

charging for water services to households, and to cover the cost of these services through the general taxation system. Water supplied to domestic users is not metered.

Industrial and commercial users do pay "local rates" (i.e. local property taxes and a *charge for water supplied* above a certain level, defined by the local authority. Large industrial users are charged on a metered basis in most instances. These charges appear to cover operating costs. A survey in 1994 revealed that in Greater Dublin industrial and commercial users received 36% of the water distributed but contributed 45% of water utility revenues. Water charges paid by industrial and commercial users generally also include a *contribution to waste water treatment* (often billed together with water supply charges). Industrial users have recently been required to contribute to the capital cost of municipal treatment plants to which they discharge. These contributions, set on a marginal cost basis through negotiation between the firm and local authority, generally relate to the volume and characteristics of the waste water discharged. They vary greatly, depending on the capacity reserved for large industrial users, but globally cover about one-third of total capital costs. Local authorities can charge firms for waste water discharges even in the absence of municipal treatment. An increasing number levy industrial effluent charges. No abstraction charge designed to reflect resource scarcity is in place.

In *rural areas*, supply of water through Group Water Schemes is supported by government grants. Farmers receive *direct payments* as part of the Rural Environmental Protection Scheme (REPS), operated under the 1992 EU Agri-Environmental Regulations, to support various measures directly aimed at various aspects of environmental protection including water quality protection. For example, they must *prepare a nutrient management plan; protect all watercourses and wells* from the impacts of grazing animals and slurry spreading; and *cease using herbicides, other pesticides and fertilisers* near waterways. By the end of 1999 there were over 45 000 "REPS farmers", accounting for more than one-third of agricultural land. To prevent nutrient pollution of watercourses, farmers can also receive capital grants for animal housing and slurry storage facilities under the Control of Farmyard Pollution Scheme (CFPS) and the Farm Improvement Programme (FIP).

Funding and expenditure

Local authorities are the main providers of both *drinking water and waste water treatment services*. Funding of these services comes largely from the central budget (since 1999, via the Local Government Fund) and, to a lesser extent, from water charges on industry. In the 1990s, there was heavy investment in sewerage and waste water treatment facilities to comply with the EU Urban Waste water Treatment Directive, with significant support from the EU, mainly the Cohesion Fund. Investment expenditure on public water supply and waste water treatment increased from IEP 110 million in 1994 to about 280 million in 1999. Over this period, capital costs for new water and sewerage infrastructure were met by EU grants (65-70%) and the Irish national budget (25-30%). Operational expenditure on public water supply and waste water treatment increased from IEP 138 million in 1994 to 189 million in 1999.

To date, the private sector has had very little involvement in constructing and operating water-related infrastructure. However, the Government is actively seeking *public-private partnerships* to help fund and manage new infrastructure, particularly in the light of declining EU funds from 2000. The new sewage treatment plant being constructed for Greater Dublin (Dublin Bay project, with a treatment capacity of 1.7 million population equivalent) is Ireland's first "Design, Build and Operate" project, whereby a private company will operate it for 20 years. This represents an IEP 200 million capital investment and IEP 200 million operational expenditure over 20 years.

In 1999, IEP 150 million was spent on the REPS, 45 million on the CFPS and 20 million on the FIP, including private expenditure (25% for REPS and 75% for CFPS and FIP). Of this amount, 10% can be directly associated with *expenditure on water quality protection in agriculture*. EU grants to help farmers drain their land were discontinued in the mid-1980s. Around IEP 20 million is spent each year by the Fisheries Boards to compensate farmers for land acquisition aimed at wetland protection. The Central Government meets all the costs of building and maintaining *flood relief schemes* (IEP 10 million in 1998).

3. Environmental Performance

Water quantity

Overall, Ireland has *abundant water resources* and does not face serious scarcity problems. However, *leakage from the distribution network* is very high, resulting in unnecessarily high operational costs for water supply. In *major cities*, water conservation programmes are under way to reduce "unaccounted for water" in the distribution network; in Greater Dublin, leakage was reduced from 42% in 1994 to 34% in 1999. A study is under way to examine public supplies in *smaller cities*; priority needs to be given to identifying water losses in each system, reviewing the demand/supply situation and choosing cost-effective responses.

Existing *flood schemes* in rural areas are being maintained. In expanding urban areas, there is a need to link better land use planning and flood hazard management to ensure that new developments are not sited in flood prone areas.

Drinking water supply

Efforts are needed to improve *drinking water quality*, so as to meet the requirements of the 1980 EU Drinking Water Directive. Currently as many as 400 000 people (12% of the population) may receive drinking water of substandard quality, particularly in rural areas. Financial transfers to Group Water Schemes have substantially increased in recent years, and quality improvement of water supplies is given high priority in the context of forthcoming strategic rural water plans. These plans will form the basis for considerable investment over the period 2000-06. They are expected to serve as the blueprint for developing rural water supplies, in a spirit of partnership between the public and private water supply sectors. However, it is estimated that 12 500 households will never be reached by piped supply systems and will therefore continue to depend on wells. Particular attention should be given to the risk of contamination of water supplies by pathogens (e.g. cryptosporidium, giardia) in catchments that receive slurry.

Following a 1997 decision, *Ireland does not price public domestic water services*: water supply and waste water services are provided free of charge to households. Until 1997, households paid a flat fee for supplied water as part of local property taxes. Irish water fees were the lowest among EU countries, even when expressed in terms of purchasing power parities (USD 0.45 per cubic metre in 1992 on national average), reflecting large State subsidisation. Industrial and commercial users have been paying volumetric charges with a higher unit rate (in PPP terms, USD 0.68 per cubic metre in Dublin in 1995). In the short term, the marginal costs of a "rational" pricing system (which would inevitably require domestic metering) probably outweigh the benefits. In the medium to long term (five to ten years), the most cost-effective measure would probably be to reduce leakage. However, in the longer term there should be charges on water services according to the quantity used, thus applying the User Pays Principle. In the meantime, in larger urban centres such as Cork and Dublin, domestic meters should be installed as opportunities arise, such as in new developments and when water mains are replaced. With increased per capita income (now above the EU average), many households are moving to the suburbs of large cities, generating demand for new water supply services as well as other utilities and transport services.

Water quality and aquatic ecosystems

Environmental conditions and trends

Most *groundwater* used for drinking water has low nitrate levels. There are no designated nitrate sensitive areas in Ireland. Faecal contamination of groundwater used for drinking water needs to be addressed through a combination of better well protection and improved waste water treatment.

The generally satisfactory situation of *Irish surface water quality* is threatened by the increasing occurrence of slight and moderate pollution of the river system. That trend, observed since the late 1970s, mainly relates to *eutrophication*; a similar situation exists for lakes. This is mainly due nowadays to developments in agriculture, including a substantial increase in livestock density, with cattle accounting for 85% of total livestock manure production. Moreover, there are indications of an upward trend in nitrate levels in water bodies in the south-east, where most of the arable farming is carried out. Serious chronic pollution, which has never been widespread, was reduced to around 1% of river length through improved domestic and industrial sewage treatment. However, pollution episodes due to direct entry of *farm wastes and discharges from other sources into water* have often led to fish kills and remain a problem. Available data suggest that water contains little in the way of *toxic substances*. Agriculture is the largest single contributor to the phosphorus load on fresh waters, followed by households and industry. Progress with domestic and industrial sewage treatment highlights the need to implement measures to address pollution from farming activities.

Although systems for monitoring river and lake water quality are well developed, information on aquatic ecosystems is not routinely collected, reflecting the focus of stream and river management on water quality. To achieve *ecological objectives*, and particularly to support trout and salmon fisheries, a broader approach is needed, including collection of information on habitat factors such as light, bank and hydraulic conditions, aimed at halting the current gradual decline in river ecosystem health. Clear objectives have not been established for coastal management, estuaries and groundwater. The EPA has issued proposals to develop *Environmental Quality Objectives* (EQO), which may need to be reviewed in the light of the EU Framework Directive on Water Policy. To help focus water management, the development of EQO with an extended coverage of ecosystem aspects would be desirable.

Cost-effectiveness and instruments

Ireland has initiated an extensive programme to establish comprehensive water quality monitoring and management based on river and lake catchments. Since 1997, DOELG has promoted a *national catchment-based strategy against eutrophication*. Significant catchment-based initiatives are in place or under way, supported by the national programme of capital investment in upgrading sewage treatment infrastructure. As many *catchment plans* have been prepared, a comprehensive review of their successes and failures should be undertaken and guidance derived on preparing and implementing catchment plans. A clearly defined agency should have the lead role in preparing and monitoring implementation of catchment plans; the EPA is well-placed to play this role.

To give strong *statutory and regulatory* underpinning to the national strategy against eutrophication, far-reaching *phosphorus regulations* were issued in 1998 aimed at incremental improvements of phosphorus concentrations in water over a ten-year period. The EPA will regularly review progress on these regulations' implementation by local authorities. Other *regulatory measures* have been taken to control farm pollution, particularly nutrient management planning and by-laws regulating certain agricultural activities.

Enforcement of regulations should nevertheless be improved. A recent farm survey in the Loughs Ree and Derg catchments indicated that manure storage systems were deficient on 70% of farms, and that 30% had inadequate facilities for containing farmyard runoff. Accountability for water quality management and clear *responsibilities* are hard to identify. There is duplication in the roles of bodies such as the EPA, County Councils and the Fisheries Board. Water legislation has evolved in an *ad hoc* manner, and there are numerous interrelated laws covering water management. Consideration should be given to *consolidating existing water legislation*. IPC licensing by the EPA should be extended to a wider range of farm activities.

Economic incentives have been introduced. Direct payments are provided to farmers engaged in environmentally friendly practices, and capital grants are awarded to help build manure storage facilities. These efforts to secure more responsible farming methods have helped reduce fertiliser use by 10% over the last five years, and have helped address the most spectacular cases of pollution. However, introducing *economic instruments* as part of pollution prevention and control policies might be considered and their cost-effectiveness analysed. A general excise tax on fertilisers would be easy to administer, but could lead to substantial imports from Northern Ireland or Great Britain. A fine on nutrient surplus (based on farm fertilisation accounts) would be consistent with the Polluter Pays Principle. Voluntary contracts between fishermen and farmers would be of mutual benefit to protect rivers and lakes at risk.

Financing present and future efforts

Ireland has recently made progress towards achieving its *waste water treatment* objectives. Around 68% of the population was connected to sewerage and 61% to waste water treatment plant in the late 1990s (Figure 2.5). These proportions have been growing following the large investment effort made in the 1990s with EU support (Table 2.3). As most treatment is primary, Ireland still has much to do achieve the objectives of the EU Urban Waste water Directive. Large agglomerations account for over 60% of total discharges. Construction of secondary

Figure 2.5   **Population connected to public waste water treatment plant,** late 1990s[a]

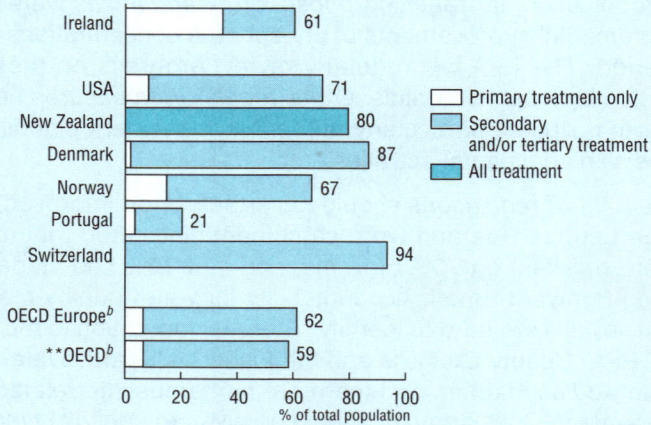

Primary treatment only
Secondary and/or tertiary treatment
All treatment

Ireland — 61
USA — 71
New Zealand — 80
Denmark — 87
Norway — 67
Portugal — 21
Switzerland — 94

OECD Europe[b] — 62
**OECD[b] — 59

% of total population

a)   Or latest available year.
b)   Secretariat estimates.
Source: OECD.

Table 2.3   **Population connected to public waste water treatment plant**
(%)

	1980	1990	1995	1997
Primary treatment	0.2	23	39	35
Secondary treatment	11	21	20	26
Tertiary treatment	0	0	0	0
Total	11.2	44	59	61

Source: OECD.

© OECD 2000

treatment schemes is well advanced at Dundalk and Drogheda, and is under way in Dublin; other schemes at Galway, Limerick, Cork and Waterford are undergoing the planning and procurement process. Nearly 75% of the 167 agglomerations with over 2 000 population equivalent (p.e.) requiring secondary treatment will be in compliance in the next few years. About 6% of total population equivalent undergoes phosphorus removal. Phosphorus reduction facilities are also being provided in a number of towns under 10 000 (p.e.), going beyond the requirements of the EU Waste water Treatment Directive.

Ireland has benefited from *substantial co-financing by the EU* to assist the development of water supply and sewerage and waste water treatment infrastructure. The bulk (60-65%) of funding of public capital investment has been provided by the EU Cohesion Fund. Ireland has also received Structural Fund assistance at regional level through the 1994-99 Operational Programme for Environmental Services (5-10%) and, for the Border region, through the Interreg II initiative (2%). The State provides the balance (25-30%). Capital provision has grown rapidly in the second part of the community support framework period: in 1999, it was more than double the 1996 figure. Public funding of such investments ranges from 100% (major projects and leakage reduction works) to 25% (small water schemes).

Industry and other non-domestic users currently contribute to *capital expenditure* on infrastructure broadly in proportion to their usage of water and waste water services; this covers about one-third of total capital costs of waste water treatment, as industry directly treats some 90% of its own sewage (self-treatment is especially common in the food processing industry). Local authorities cover *operational expenditure* with funds from commercial rates, receipts from the Local Government Fund and other miscellaneous receipts. However, operational expenditure will increase significantly in the future as new and expanded schemes are completed. A growing number of local authorities levy industrial effluent charges. Public-private partnerships will need to be developed to address Ireland's infrastructure deficit in the light of *declining EU funding*. Full implementation of the Polluter Pays Principle requires that *polluters* cover the capital and operational expenditure of waste water services.

3

AIR MANAGEMENT

1. Air Pollution Situation and Trends

Emissions of atmospheric pollutants

Since 1990, Ireland's *emissions of SO_x* have been rather stable, averaging 170 kt per year. Although there has been a decoupling from GDP growth since the mid 1980s, SO_x emissions intensity (2.5 kg/USD 1 000) remains 25% higher than the OECD Europe average (Figure 3.1); emissions per capita are 62% higher. The main sources are power stations (62%), industry (17%) and the residential and commercial sectors (14%). Emissions reductions achieved by industry (17%) and the residential and commercial sectors (28%) since 1990 have been offset by increasing emissions from power stations (8%) and transport (40%).

Emissions of NO_x since 1990 have also changed little, averaging 121 kt per year. There has been a decoupling of NO_x emissions from GDP growth since the early 1990s (Figure 3.1). NO_x emissions intensity is 5% lower than the OECD Europe average, but per capita emissions are 20% higher. The main sources are transport (49%), power stations (34%), industry (7%) and the residential and commercial sectors (6%). Transport emissions increased from 40 to 49% of total emissions between 1990 and 1998; in the same period, emissions from power stations and industry decreased by about 9% and 13%, respectively.

Emissions of CO_2 from energy use were 40 Mt in 1998, 19% above 1990. Since the late 1980s, they have grown more slowly than GDP (Figure 3.1), reflecting improvements in energy efficiency (Figure 3.2). However, CO_2 emissions per unit GDP are 11% higher than the OECD Europe average and per capita emissions are 30% higher. The major sources of CO_2 emissions are energy transformation (38%), transport (23%) and the residential and commercial sectors (24%).

Emissions of CH_4, rather stable since 1990, totalled 694 kt in 1998. The principal source of methane emissions is agriculture (78%). Also comparatively stable since 1990, *N_2O emissions* in 1998 totalled 32 kt, of which nearly 75% was

Figure 3.1   **Air pollutant emissions**

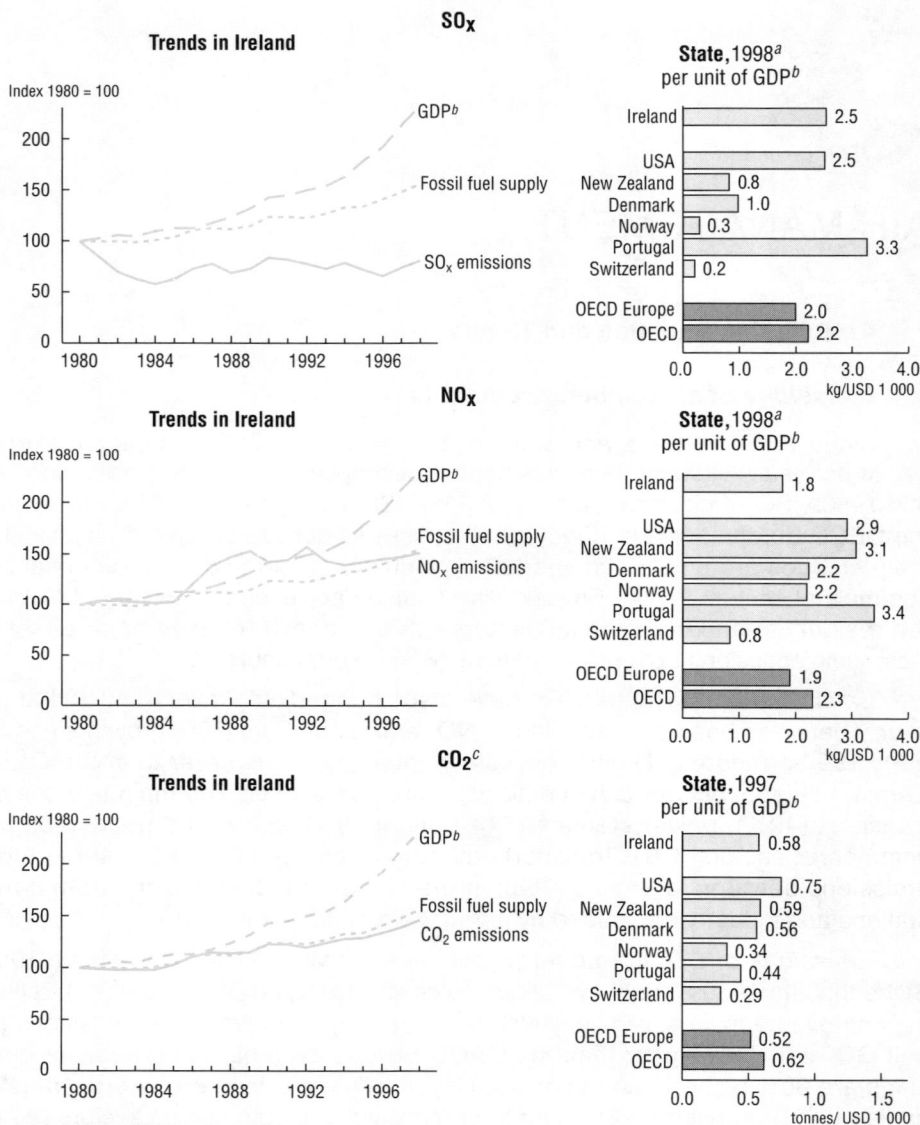

SO_X

Trends in Ireland

Index 1980 = 100

GDP[b]

Fossil fuel supply

SO_x emissions

State,1998[a]
per unit of GDP[b]

Ireland	2.5
USA	2.5
New Zealand	0.8
Denmark	1.0
Norway	0.3
Portugal	3.3
Switzerland	0.2
OECD Europe	2.0
OECD	2.2

0.0   1.0   2.0   3.0   4.0
kg/USD 1 000

NO_X

Trends in Ireland

Index 1980 = 100

GDP[b]

Fossil fuel supply

NO_x emissions

State,1998[a]
per unit of GDP[b]

Ireland	1.8
USA	2.9
New Zealand	3.1
Denmark	2.2
Norway	2.2
Portugal	3.4
Switzerland	0.8
OECD Europe	1.9
OECD	2.3

0.0   1.0   2.0   3.0   4.0
kg/USD 1 000

$CO_2{}^{c}$

Trends in Ireland

Index 1980 = 100

GDP[b]

Fossil fuel supply

CO_2 emissions

State,1997
per unit of GDP[b]

Ireland	0.58
USA	0.75
New Zealand	0.59
Denmark	0.56
Norway	0.34
Portugal	0.44
Switzerland	0.29
OECD Europe	0.52
OECD	0.62

0.0   0.5   1.0   1.5
tonnes/ USD 1 000

a) Or latest available year.
b) GDP at 1991 prices and purchasing power parities.
c) Emissions from energy use only; excludes international marine bunkers.
Source: OECD; IEA.

Figure 3.2   **Energy structure and intensity**

Energy^a per unit of GDP^b

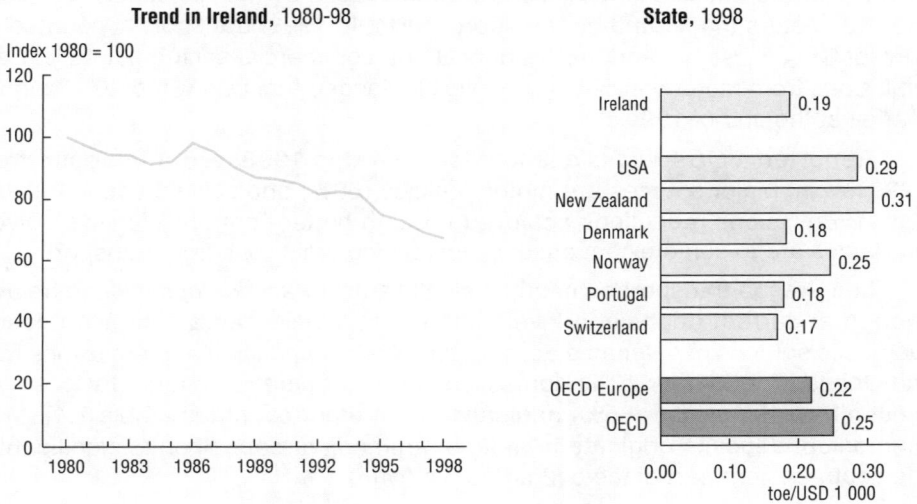

Trend in Ireland, 1980-98

Index 1980 = 100

```
120
100
 80
 60
 40
 20
  0
   1980   1983   1986   1989   1992   1995   1998
```

State, 1998

Ireland	0.19
USA	0.29
New Zealand	0.31
Denmark	0.18
Norway	0.25
Portugal	0.18
Switzerland	0.17
OECD Europe	0.22
OECD	0.25

```
0.00     0.10     0.20    0.30
                   toe/USD 1 000
```

Total final energy consumption by sector, 1998

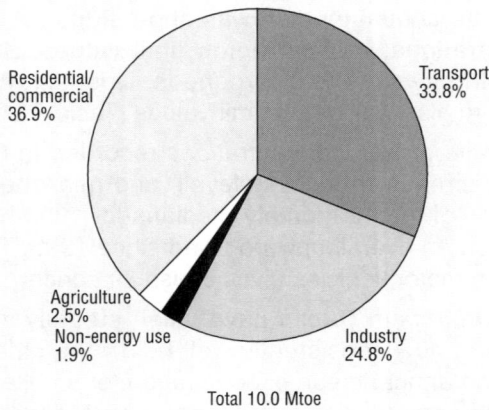

Residential/
commercial
36.9%

Transport
33.8%

Agriculture
2.5%

Non-energy use
1.9%

Industry
24.8%

Total 10.0 Mtoe

a)   Total primary energy supply.
b)   GDP at 1991 prices and purchasing power parities.
Source: OECD; IEA.

contributed by agriculture. Both CH_4 and N_2O emissions intensities are high on a per capita basis, reflecting the importance of agricultural emissions (e.g. from livestock raising).

Since 1990, *CO emissions* have dropped by about 17%, reaching 333 kt in 1998. Large emissions reductions were achieved by the residential and commercial sectors (41%) and by transport (10%). In 1998, transport accounted for 82% of CO emissions, and the residential and commercial sectors for 16%. *Lead emissions* from motor vehicles are negligible; leaded fuel was withdrawn from the market at the end of 1999.

Reported *VOCs emissions* totalled 117 kt in 1998, a 6% increase from 1990 levels. Major sources are motor vehicles (60%) and solvent use in industry (25%). Emissions reductions achieved through better control of fugitive solvent emissions are to some extent offset by increasing emissions from transport.

Long-range transport contributes significantly to *acidic deposition* in Ireland, though at current deposition levels this is not considered a significant issue. Domestic sources of sulphates account for 34% of deposition and emissions from the United Kingdom for 40%; domestic sources of nitrates amount to 15%, with most nitrate deposition (85%) originating from other countries (Table 7.4). Most ammonium deposits originate in Ireland; ammonium deposition is significant in the south-eastern part of the country (0.5 g N/m^2).

Ambient air quality

Ambient SO_2 concentrations in Dublin and Cork largely stabilised in the 1990s. In 1998, the annual median was about 20μg/m³ in both cities; even winter peak concentrations were far below limit values. SO_2 concentrations recorded at local authority sites (e.g. Drogheda, Dundalk, Waterford, Wexford, Limerick, Galway) were also well below limit values (Table 3.1).

The 98th percentile of *NO_x concentrations* recorded in Dublin in 1998 was 185 μg/m³, a slight increase from 1990 levels and near the limit value. In the period 1990-98, seven of the 12 monthly medians for 1998 were the highest on record; there has been an overall upward trend since 1993. The recent increase in NO_x emissions from motor vehicles gives cause for concern.

Smoke concentrations in Dublin have fallen steadily and dramatically in recent years. They are now consistently well below the strictest limit value for smoke (80 μg/m³). The annual mean concentration for smoke in 1998 was about 10 μg/m³, an 83% decrease relative to 1990 and a 95% decrease compared with the mid 1980s. A similar trend has been seen in Cork since 1994, when smoke control legislation was introduced. Smoke levels at local authority sites are all well below limit values, with winter means generally under 30 μg/m³ and the 98th percentile of daily means less than 80 μg/m³. Levels of smoke recorded at

Electricity Supply Board (ESB) sites are also quite low (annual mean less than 20 $\mu g/m^3$; 98th percentile less than 20 $\mu g/m^3$).

Daily *PM_{10} concentrations* in the Greater Dublin Area in the mid 1990s approached or exceeded the proposed EU daily limit value of 50 $\mu g/m^3$. Throughout the city centre, weekly average levels ranged from 50 to 138 $\mu g/m^3$; high levels were also measured along major traffic arteries.

VOCs concentrations are not yet subject to routine monitoring in Ireland. However, a 1997 survey of BTX concentrations in Dublin revealed moderate annual average ambient concentrations (benzene: 5 $\mu g/m^3$; toluene: 12 $\mu g/m^3$; xylenes: 15 $\mu g/m^3$). Measured BTX concentrations were strongly correlated with proximity to motor vehicles.

Dublin's *tropospheric ozone levels* are generally well below EU threshold levels. The annual median of eight-hour means has been rather stable since 1991, varying between 35 and 50 $\mu g/m^3$. Exceedances occur in summer; in 1997, the

Table 3.1 **Ambient air quality limits applied in Ireland**

	Parameter	Limit value	International reference
SO_2	Annual median of daily values Winter median of daily values	120 $\mu g/m^3$, if smoke < 40 $\mu g/m^3$ 80 $\mu g/m^3$, if smoke > 40 $\mu g/m^3$ 180 $\mu g/m^3$, if smoke < 60 $\mu g/m^3$ 130 $\mu g/m^3$, if smoke > 60 $\mu g/m^3$	EU Directive 80/779/EEC
Black smoke	Annual median of daily values Winter median of daily values	80 $\mu g/m^3$ 130 $\mu g/m^3$	EU Directive 80/779/EEC

NO_2	Annual median of 1-hr means
	P_{98} of all daily mean values
	  measured throughout
	  the year
		50 $\mu g/m^3$
		200 $\mu g/m^3$
			EU Directive 85/203/EEC

O_3	1-hr mean
	8-hr mean
		180 $\mu g/m^3$, population information
		  level
		360 $\mu g/m^3$, population warning
		  level
		110 $\mu g/m^3$, health protection level
			EU Directive 92/72/EEC

CO	1-hr max. 8-hr max.	30 mg/m^3 10 mg/m^3	WHO air quality guideline
Lead	Annual mean	2 $\mu g/m^3$	EU Directive 82/884/EEC

Source: DOELG; OECD.

EU limit for human health protection (110 µg/m^3 over an eight-hour period) was exceeded on ten days.

2. Responses

Objectives

Ireland's *1997 Sustainable Development Strategy* has several air quality management objectives. These include: maintaining or improving local air quality, particularly in urban areas; participating in international actions to reduce air emissions; and actively supporting international actions concerning climate change, ozone depletion and transboundary air pollution.

Air quality standards for SO_2, NO_x, O_3, smoke and lead are based on EU limit and guideline values. Air quality is also assessed with respect to WHO guideline values (e.g. for CO) (Table 3.1).

Ireland has established *reduction targets for SO_x and NO_x* emissions through several international agreements. Under the Oslo Protocol (1994), it committed to maintaining national SO_2 emissions below 155 kt until 2000; under the Sofia Protocol (1988), it committed to stabilising national NO_x emissions at 105 kt by 1994. Under the Gothenburg Protocol (1999), Ireland is committed to limiting national SO_x emissions to 42 kt (76% reduction from 1990 level) and national NO_x emissions to 65 kt (43% reduction from 1990 level) by 2010. It has not signed the Geneva Protocol (1991) on VOCs emissions. The EU directive on large combustion sources establishes annual emissions ceilings for SO_x (124 kt) and NO_x (50 kt).

Ireland has adopted goals related to *reduction of greenhouse gas emissions*. The 1993 National Strategy to Abate CO_2 Emissions aimed at ensuring that emissions of CO_2 in 2000 did not exceed 1990 levels by more than 20%. In the framework of the Kyoto Protocol, Ireland is committed to limit growth in national GHG emissions, such that in the period 2008-12 its national emissions do not exceed 1990 levels by over 13% (Chapter 7).

The 1995 Renewable Energy Strategy sets the objective of *increasing use of renewable fuels* for electricity generation, to account for 10% of national generating capacity by the end of 1999 and 14% by 2010. The 1999 Green Paper on Sustainable Energy sets an even more ambitious target (16.6% of generating capacity) for 2005. As an EU member, Ireland's commitments in the 1990s included making *significant fuel quality improvements* and phasing out leaded petrol by the end of 1999.

Measures to prevent and control air pollution

The *Air Pollution Act* (1987) empowered DOELG to issue ambient air quality standards and specify air emission limits for certain sources. It also provided local authorities with wide-ranging enforcement powers relating to air pollution, including the power to adopt local air quality management plans. The *Environmental Protection Agency Act* (1992) created the EPA as an independent statutory body charged with implementing integrated pollution control (IPC) licensing. Regulatory responsibility for eligible activities is being transferred from local authorities to the EPA on a phased basis. Activities which are not IPC licensed remain under the jurisdiction of local authorities.

Regulatory measures

A 1990 *ban on bituminous coal* prohibits its marketing, sale and distribution in Dublin. A similar ban was imposed in Cork in 1995, and subsequently in ten other urban areas including Dundalk, Drogheda, Limerick, Arklow and Wexford. This measure has greatly reduced urban smoke concentrations.

Since 1994, over 300 *integrated pollution control (IPC) licenses* have been issued by the EPA. By 2002, all new and existing facilities with significant polluting potential are to be subject to IPC licensing. In 2000, IPC licenses were required in particular for chemical plants and gas- and oil-fired power plants, boilers and furnaces. Existing peat-fired power plants and boilers will be subject to IPC licensing in 2002. Companies licensed under the IPC scheme are required to operate an environmental management system (Chapter 5).

Building regulations for new homes were revised in 1991 to strengthen thermal insulation standards. By 1996, nearly 150 000 houses (approximately 12% of total housing stock) had been built to the new specifications. Further revisions in 1997 introduced an optional energy rating system for houses. Under the EU's THERMIE programme, 58 houses have been built in five Irish cities to demonstrate the cost-effectiveness of best practice "low-energy, low-CO_2" building techniques.

Since 1970, conformance with EU *vehicle emissions standards* has been a requirement for first-time registration of all petrol- and diesel-fuelled vehicles, and for most light and heavy duty commercial vehicles (Chapter 6). In the case of petrol-fuelled vehicles, emissions limits for CO, NO_x and VOCs entail a (de facto) three-way catalytic converter requirement. Ireland enforces EU *motor vehicle fuel standards*. The sulphur content of diesel fuel was reduced to 0.2% in 1994 and 0.05% in 1996. The phase-out of leaded fuel was completed in 1999. However, comprehensive emissions testing of in-use vehicles has been delayed, with implementation dating from 2000 (Chapter 6).

Economic instruments

Under the *energy audit* scheme, the Irish Energy Centre (IEC) provides grants to industrial, commercial and institutional energy users. They subsidise up to 40% (or a maximum of IEP 5 000) of the cost of energy audits carried out to identify means of enhancing operational energy efficiency. In 1997, grants totalling IEP 200 000 were awarded.

A *household heating fuels subsidy* (IEP 3 per week) is provided by the Department of Social, Community, and Family Affairs to low-income households in areas subject to a bituminous coal ban. This payment is to compensate for the cost of switching to smokeless fuels, as mandated by the bituminous coal ban. Since 1990, state *housing grants* available to purchasers in the Dublin area have been contingent on houses being equipped with smokeless heating facilities. Liquefied petroleum gas (LPG) used for heating or industrial purposes benefits from a lower *fuel excise tax* than that on other fuels (Table 5.5).

The *vehicle registration tax (VRT)* on first-time registration is calculated as a function of engine size (Table 5.5). A standard *21% VAT* is levied on all vehicle purchases. All vehicles pay an *annual motor vehicle tax* differentiated to favour smaller engines. Electric cars and those with small engine capacity (less than 1 000 cc) pay a flat tax of IEP 98; the tax on goods vehicles is calculated as a function of unladen weight (Table 5.5).

Lower *excise tax on motor vehicle fuels* is applied to diesel and LPG (Table 5.5). Irish *motor vehicle fuel prices* are considerably lower than those in the UK. In 1998, the price of unleaded premium in Ireland was 14% lower than the pump price in the UK; for diesel fuel, the Irish pump price was 30% lower than in the UK (Table 6.3).

A *vehicle scrapping programme* implemented between 1995 and 1997 was aimed at reducing the number of old passenger cars. A lower VRT for new vehicles was an incentive to scrap old ones (Chapter 6). About 61 000 vehicles (some 6% of the fleet) were scrapped.

Monitoring and reporting

Air quality monitoring in Ireland has historically concentrated on smoke and SO_2. These are measured at 65 sampling stations operated by 17 local authorities, and at 21 sites operated by the Electricity Supply Board (ESB). Monitoring by local authorities and the ESB takes place in small towns or rural areas near power stations. Reflecting population distribution, monitoring capacity is concentrated in Dublin. Monitoring of NO_x, VOCs, O_3 and PM_{10} is fairly limited. NO_x is monitored at three stations (two in Dublin and one in Cork) and CO at one (in Dublin). Lead concentrations are measured at seven stations and PM_{10} at six (five in Dublin and one in Cork). Ozone monitoring takes place at six sites, three urban and three rural.

Industrial reporting is required of all industries licensed through the IPC system. Companies must publish annual environmental performance reports, including estimations of air emissions when relevant. The IEC has implemented *voluntary audit and reporting* initiatives, such as the Annual Self-Audit and Statement of Energy Accounts programmes, to promote energy efficiency by intensive energy users. Under the Self-Audit scheme, participants have recorded an annual Energy Performance Index reduction of 3%; avoided emissions were estimated at 150 000 tonnes of CO_2.

Investment and expenditure for air pollution prevention and control

Since 1994, Ireland's *Energy Efficiency Investment Support Scheme* has provided IEP 7.1 million in grant assistance to industrial, commercial and residential energy users for investment in energy-efficient technologies. Total IEC funding between 1994 and 1999, largely used to promote voluntary energy efficiency approaches, was IEP 40 million.

The reported *annual cost of the household fuels subsidy* in 1998, under the ban on bituminous coal, was IEP 8.9 million. Nearly 70% was distributed to Dublin area households.

Since 1992, Ireland has invested IEP 7 million in *low-NO_x burners* for three boilers at the coal-fired Moneypoint station, the country's largest power plant. In the budgetary period 1998-2005, IEP 70 million in investment has been programmed for the Whitegate refinery, largely to meet the latest environmentally based EU requirements for automotive oil fuel. The bulk of this investment was completed in 2000.

Air quality management and the energy sector

The *Department of Public Enterprise (DPE)* is responsible for Ireland's general energy policy. Created in 1994 at the joint initiative of the DPE and industry, the Irish Energy Centre is responsible for implementing energy efficiency policies. Two regional IEC energy offices in Sligo and Cork provide training and information and promote voluntary energy conservation measures. In 1999, the DPE issued a Green Paper on Sustainable Energy that places high priority on development of renewable energy sources and improvement of energy efficiency.

Energy intensity

The *energy intensity* of the Irish economy fell by 22% between 1990 and 1998, reaching a level (0.19 toe/USD 1 000) 14% below the OECD Europe average (Figure 3.2). The greatest gains in energy efficiency were made in industry, followed by the residential and transport sectors. In the same period, total final energy consumption increased by 29%, largely due to increased motor vehicle use and electricity consumption. *Final energy consumption* is dominated by the residential and commercial sectors (37%), transport (34%) and industry (25%) (Figure 3.2). Electricity consumption has increased by almost 50% since 1990; residential and commercial users account for about two-thirds of consumption and industry for the remainder.

Average *energy efficiency* of Ireland's *electricity production* is 36%, about 8% below the EU average. In 1997, ESB's power generation capacity was 4 120 MW; 1 210 MW (30% of the total) had been installed since 1986. Additional capacity of at least 800 MW is projected to be required by 2005. Primary energy supply used to produce electricity in 1998 consisted of coal (33%), natural gas (29%), oil (24%) and peat (11%). Since known domestic sources of natural gas are nearing exhaustion, the Government is committed to continued peat use as a way to reduce energy dependence. A new peat-fired plant (120 MW) is to be commissioned in 2001, consuming 1 million tonnes of peat per year. Energy efficiency of peat-fired power plants in Ireland is currently only 23%, but the new plant is planned to be significantly more efficient.

Energy supply

Oil accounts for *55% of total primary energy supply* (TPES), gas 21%, coal 15% and peat 7%. Combustible renewables and waste make up the remainder. Overall, Ireland depends on imports for about 82% of energy supply. The only *indigenous gas production*, from the Kinsale and Ballycotton fields, will be exhausted by 2005. Barring discovery of new fields, and given rapidly growing demand for gas (8% annual increase since 1992), gas imports are expected to grow in coming years. An interconnector with the United Kingdom, completed in 1995, ensures natural gas supply. In 1999, *renewables* contributed less than 3% of TPES.

Peat accounts for about 33% of *domestic energy production*. Its use in power generation is expected to peak with the commissioning of the new peat-fired plant in 2001. The new plant's construction is supported by a EUR 26 million grant from the EU Economic Infrastructure Operational Programme, amounting to 20% of its capital costs. *Bord na Móna* (BNM), a public limited company, harvests peat on 88 000 hectares (over 7% of Ireland's total peat reserve) and supplies the five main peat-fired plants with about 5 million tonnes per year. The remaining working life of BNM's bogs is estimated at some 30 years. Since 1996, BNM has received government subsidies of IEP 108 million to help repay unsustained debts. These subsidies have helped lower the price of milled peat sold to the ESB for electricity generation, which has fallen from IEP 19 to IEP 15 per tonne.

Energy prices

Electricity prices for households and industry are roughly equivalent to those in neighbouring countries, but are 5-9% lower than the OECD Europe average (Table 3.2). *Increases* in electricity prices were implemented in 1996 and 1997. Electricity bills rose by 2% for households, 1.5% for industry and 1% for commercial customers. An average 3% increase proposed in 1998 was not approved by the Government, due to the ESB's unexpectedly high profitability in the late 1990s.

The price of *natural gas* in Ireland is 15-20% higher than in neighbouring countries. At 1998 prices and exchange rates, the price for industry was 20% higher than the OECD Europe average (Table 3.2), reflecting Ireland's import

Table 3.2   **Energy prices in selected OECD countries,** 1998

	Electricity		Oil		Natural gas	
	Industry[a] (USD/kWh)	Households[b] (USD/kWh)	Industry[a, c] (USD/toe)	Households[b, d] (USD/1 000 litres)	Industry[a] (USD/toe)	Households[b] (USD/10[7] kcal)
Ireland	0.060	0.12	166.0	352.6	190.6	425.8
France	0.047	0.12	108.3	303.7	161.6	394.1
Germany	0.067	0.14	..	201.5	210.9[e]	360.7[e]
Greece	0.050	0.13	..	473.8	not appl.	not appl.
Netherlands	0.062	0.12	..	360.9	136.7	342.5
Portugal	0.094	0.22	149.7	808.8	..	not appl.
United Kingdom	0.065	0.11	134.4	190.1	120.8	304.4
OECD Europe	0.066	0.13	135.5	296.5	158.8	432.9[e]
OECD	0.051	0.10	137.7	283.9	134.8	357.7[e]
Irish price/ OECD Europe	91%	95%	123%	119%	120%	101%[c]
Irish price/ OECD	116%	123%	121%	124%	141%	122%[e]

a) At current prices and exchange rates.
b) Adjusted with purchasing power parities.
c) High-sulphur oil.
d) Light fuel oil.
e) 1997 data.
Source: IEA-OECD.

dependence. Gas from domestic fields has historically been supplied at lower prices than those for North Sea gas; recent price increases reflect the declining importance of domestic sources.

The price of *oil for heating or industrial use* in 1998 was about 25% higher than in neighbouring countries, again reflecting Ireland's import dependence (Table 3.2). However, at 1998 prices and exchange rates the price of *diesel fuel* was 30% lower than in the UK (Table 6.3). Adjusted for purchasing power parities, the price of unleaded premium motor vehicle fuel in Ireland was about 10% lower than the average for France, Germany, the Netherlands and the United Kingdom. In 1998, the excise duty on leaded (phased out at the end of 1999) and super unleaded was increased by 4 pence per litre.

Air quality management and the transport sector

The *transport sector* is a *major source of air emissions*, accounting for 82% of CO, 49% of NO$_x$, 5% of SO$_2$ (Table 6.1) and 23% of CO$_2$. The share of energy use by the transport sector (34% of TFC), roughly equal to the OECD Europe average, is growing rapidly. Road travel is the dominant *domestic passenger transport* mode, accounting for 96% of passenger-kilometres (Chapter 6). With continued rapid growth of the road vehicle fleet, road transport's share of air emissions can be expected to continue to increase.

The *Operational Programme for Transport* (OPT) defined investment priorities for 1994-99 aimed at improving energy efficiency and the operational speed of rail transport, and at further developing public transport. Infrastructure improvements intended to alleviate congestion in Dublin (e.g. completion of the urban ring road and port tunnel, synchronisation of the traffic light system) have been actively pursued. EIA is routinely and effectively applied to all major transport projects. Since 1990, numerous measures have been implemented to improve vehicles' emissions performance (Chapter 6).

3. Environmental Performance

Air management

Air quality objectives

In *rural areas and small towns*, measurements indicate very satisfactory air quality. In *Dublin and Cork*, ambient air quality has improved in terms of smoke, lead and SO$_x$ since 1990. The smoky smog of the 1980s has been eliminated through the ban on bituminous coal. Lead is no longer of concern following the phase-out of leaded fuel. Ambient SO$_x$ concentrations are stable at levels well below regulatory limits.

However, available information on PM_{10}, NO_x and O_3 concentrations showed increases in the late 1990s, with levels approaching or exceeding existing or proposed limit values. A recent study of toxic VOCs (BTX) in Dublin detected concentrations close to the suggested EU limit value, particularly near roads, signalling a potential future concern. Overall, monitoring of these pollutants is very limited and should be developed on a routine basis, particularly in major urban areas.

Air emissions objectives

Since 1990, there has been a weak *decoupling of emissions of SO_x and NO_x from economic growth*, which can be attributed to economic changes (e.g. the relative and rapid dematerialisation of production associated with development of the pharmaceutical, computer and other industries), energy changes (e.g. greater market penetration by natural gas) and environmental changes (e.g. stricter vehicle emissions standards, installation of low-NO_x burners at power plants). However, the economic boom has also driven a large increase in electricity production and changes in consumption patterns (higher motorisation, increased commuting associated with increased urban sprawl) that have begun to erode earlier gains.

Per capita air pollutant emissions (kg/per capita) are considerably higher than the average for OECD Europe. SO_x emissions exceed the per capita average by 62%, NO_x by 20% and CO_2 by 30%. While the emissions intensity of the Irish economy (kg/USD 1 000) is slightly lower than the OECD Europe average for NO_x, it exceeds it by 25% for SO_x and by 11% for CO_2.

Ireland's overall *performance in meeting its emission commitments is not satisfactory.* The recent upsurge in SO_x emissions from power stations (37% increase since 1996, reaching 112 kt in 1998) raises the question of how much longer Ireland will respect the 124 kt emission ceiling set by the EU's large combustion plant directive, though a voluntary agreement made with the Electricity Supply Board (ESB) in 2000 is expected to reduce SO_x emissions from the energy sector. Since 1993, *SO_x emissions* have consistently exceeded the year 2000 target set under the Oslo Protocol. *NO_x emissions* have exceeded the target set under the Sofia Protocol (105.4 kt) every year since 1990, increasing by 6% between 1990 and 1998. Transport's contribution to NO_x emissions has grown by nearly 10% since 1990, a trend likely to continue. In 1999, Ireland committed under the Gothenburg Protocol to reduce SO_x emissions to 24%, and those of NO_x to 57%, of their 1990 levels by 2010. If its commitments are to be taken seriously, *additional measures* aimed at limiting emissions of these pollutants are clearly and urgently needed.

Emissions of CO_2 are 11% higher per unit of GDP than the average for OECD Europe. They will likely exceed national and international commitments (Chapter 7). Energy-related CO_2 emissions have increased by 19% since 1990, with the share of CO_2 from electricity generation reaching 38% in 1997. Despite the efforts of the Irish Energy Centre (IEC) to promote energy conservation, additional measures will be necessary if emissions are to be limited to internationally agreed targets.

Pollution control measures

In the 1990s, Ireland implemented a number of *regulatory measures* aimed at reducing emissions from the residential/commercial, transport and industrial sectors. Thermal insulation standards for new housing were strengthened in the 1990s, and nearly 15% of the existing housing stock now conforms to these higher standards. Following relevant EU directives, all new petrol-fuelled cars have three-way catalytic converters and fuel quality has improved, leading to reduced unitary vehicular emissions. Leaded fuel phase-out was completed in 1999. The bituminous coal bans implemented in 12 urban areas have achieved drastic urban smoke emissions reductions. The IPC licensing programme administered by the EPA for large fixed sources of pollution, initiated in 1994, is strengthening and harmonising best practices for inspection and enforcement on a country-wide basis. As local authorities maintain their regulatory responsibility for smaller sources, improving their skills and resources should also be a priority, possibly entailing regular staff exchanges with the IPC programme.

Some *economic instruments* are used to support air quality management objectives, particularly relating to transport. A range of taxes and charges applied to motor vehicles partially internalise external environmental costs. However, a better balance should be sought between instruments oriented towards vehicle ownership and vehicle use (Chapter 6). As motor vehicle fuel prices in Ireland are considerably lower than those of its nearest neighbour, a fuel tax increase could be considered. The IEC has used subsidies and grants effectively on a small scale to promote industrial and residential/commercial energy efficiency. Continued subsidisation of peat use for electricity production should be re-evaluated.

Overall, public and private *environmental expenditure* for air pollution prevention and control remains very small (a small percentage of total PAC expenditure) compared to most OECD countries, and compared to expenditure on waste water collection and treatment in Ireland.

Integration of air pollution concerns into sectoral policies

The *energy intensity* (i.e. energy use per unit of GDP) of the Irish economy has fallen by 22% since 1990 and is 14% lower than the average for OECD Europe. This improvement, largely the product of economic transformation towards sectors with lower energy intensity, is rather fragile; steep increases in demand for electricity and for personal mobility will soon undermine the trend without strong efficiency improvement efforts.

The IEC has implemented several voluntary programmes, mostly aimed at the industrial and residential/commercial sectors; with a total budget of IEP 40 million (1994-99), they have produced approximately a 1% reduction of national CO_2 emissions. The most effective programmes, measured by savings in CO_2 emissions, have been the Energy Efficiency Support Scheme (100 000 tonnes per year in avoided emissions), domestic sector programmes (75 000 tonnes per year) and the Self-Audit Programme (68 000 tonnes per year). To achieve further energy efficiency improvements of the magnitude needed to conform to international commitments relating to *emissions of greenhouse gases*, Ireland will need to develop additional, larger-scale measures to reinforce those already in place. Decision-making should give clear consideration to technical feasibility, as well as to cost-benefit analyses of the options.

Energy supply is dominated by imported oil and gas. Security of energy supply is therefore a concern. Continued use of peat as fuel is often justified on energy security grounds, though it appears to be maintained more for socioeconomic reasons. Energy policies are not adequately co-ordinated with policies for peat bog conservation (Chapter 7). While the Government has sought to stimulate development of *renewables and co-generation* in recent years, concrete results have been lacking; in 1999, renewables contributed less than 3% of TPES, compared to the 10% target established in the 1995 Renewable Energy Strategy.

In the *transport sector*, well-established EIA procedures are routinely applied in project assessment (Chapter 6). Implementation of wide-ranging traffic management measures in the Dublin region (environmental traffic cells, parking management, dedicated bus corridors) should help reduce emissions associated with congestion. Further development of public transport should be given high priority in both Dublin and Cork, and its development fully integrated into long-term land use planning.

4

WASTE MANAGEMENT

1. Current Situation and Trends

Ireland has experienced *significant increases in waste generation* in recent years. In 1998, a total of about 60 million tonnes of waste was produced (an increase of over 42% since 1995). There were 45 million tonnes of agricultural waste, 12 million tonnes of industrial non-hazardous waste, 2 million tonnes of municipal waste and 1 million tonnes of other waste. The main waste management issues relate to municipal and industrial waste.

In 1995, the EPA published Ireland's first comprehensive *waste management database*. An updated report for 1998 was published in 2000. These reports distinguish three main *waste types*: agricultural, industrial and municipal. Legal definitions (e.g. waste, hazardous waste, recovery, disposal) are directly transposed from relevant EU legislation (European Waste Catalogue and Hazardous Waste List).

Municipal waste accounts for about 13% of non-agricultural waste. It comprises waste from households (59%), commercial activities (37%) and street cleaning (4%). The quantity of municipal waste collected by, or on behalf of, local authorities *doubled* between 1984 and 1998. Municipal waste generation now amounts to some 560 kg per inhabitant per year (Figure 4.1). A large part (about one-third) of household waste consists of organic materials (Table 4.1). The proportion of packaging materials, especially plastics, is increasing. The proportion of paper is higher in the urban waste stream. Some 94% of municipal waste is collected through an organised and regular service; the level of service is lower in rural areas. The share of private collection has been growing (it increased from one-third in 1995 to over half in 1998). However, waste collection remains entirely public in the Dublin and Cork Corporations. Most municipal waste (over 90%) is sent to landfill (Figure 4.2).

Nearly three-quarters of non-agricultural waste is generated by industry. *Industrial non-hazardous waste* is mainly made up of manufacturing (food products, chemicals and chemical products), mining, and construction and demolition

Figure 4.1   **Municipal waste generation,**[a] late 1990s

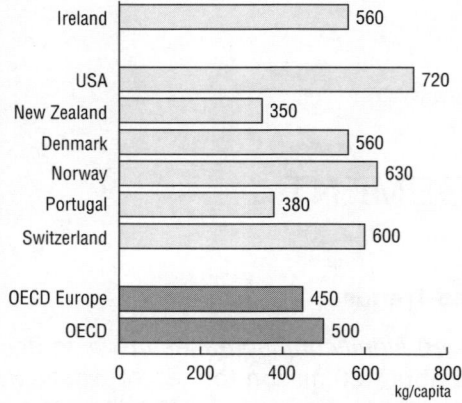

Country	kg/capita
Ireland	560
USA	720
New Zealand	350
Denmark	560
Norway	630
Portugal	380
Switzerland	600
OECD Europe	450
OECD	500

0   200   400   600   800
kg/capita

a) In interpreting national figures, it should be borne in mind that survey methods and definitions of municipal waste may
    vary from one country to another. According to the definition used by the OECD, municipal waste is waste collected
    by or for municipalities and includes household, bulky and commercial waste and similar waste handled at the same
    facilities.
Source: OECD.

Figure 4.2   **Disposal of municipal waste,** late 1990s[a]

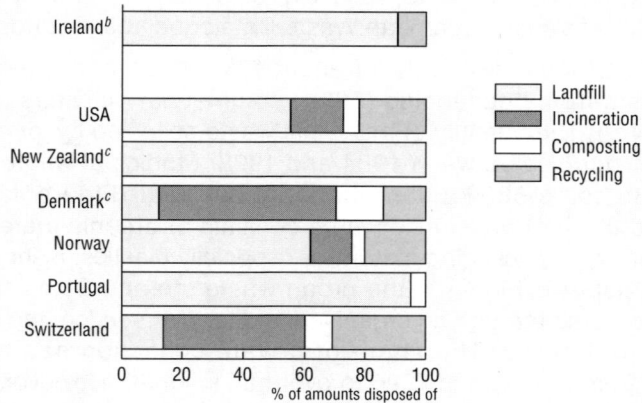

Ireland[b]
USA
New Zealand[c]
Denmark[c]
Norway
Portugal
Switzerland

Landfill
Incineration
Composting
Recycling

0   20   40   60   80   100
% of amounts disposed of

a) Or latest available year.
b) 1998 data referring to total municipal waste collected.
c) Household waste only.
Source: OECD.

waste. It *increased* by 56% between 1995 and 1998, reflecting greater industrial activity, the opening of two large mines for metal production, and the construction boom. Recovery of industrial waste has increased significantly (from 20% in 1995 to 30% in 1998); the percentage of waste sent to disposal is especially high in the mining and alumina processing industries. Construction and demolition waste is handled together with municipal waste and is generally sent to communal landfills.

Other types of waste, mainly dredge spoils and municipal liquid waste, amounted to less than 2 million tonnes in 1998. Dredge spoils are produced for the most part during harbour development and maintenance operations and are usually disposed of at sea. Sewage sludge from septic tanks serving households in some rural areas is collected by private enterprises whose activities are not controlled. While most of the sludge drains into sewer systems, part goes to land-fill since the capacity of waste water treatment plants is insufficient to treat it. This situation is evolving (Chapter 3). The 3 000 tonnes of hospital waste produced annually incorporates both hazardous and non-hazardous categories.

Nearly three-quarters of total waste originates from *agriculture*. This is consistent with the extent and importance of farming in Ireland. In 1983, cattle, pig and poultry farming produced nearly 20 million tonnes of slurry. That figure *increased* to about 42 million tonnes in 1998, with an additional 2.5 million tonnes of silage effluent. Other types of waste arising in the agricultural sector include unclean water, dead animals, agro-chemicals, sheep dips, waste oil and farm

Table 4.1 **Composition of household waste in Ireland**
(%)

	Urban areas		Rural areas	
	1995	1998	1995	1998
Paper	23	22	16	16
Plastic	10	12	10	11
Textile	2	3	4	3
Glass	5	5	5	6
Metal	4	3	3	4
Decomposing organic	40	32	29	34
Other inorganic	16	23	33	26
Total	100	100	100	100

Source: EPA.

plastics. The agricultural sector is by far the greatest producer of organic waste, with impacts on surface and groundwater quality (Chapter 3).

In 1998, an estimated 370 000 tonnes of *hazardous waste* was generated by industry (70%), agriculture (10%), services (10%) and other sources (10%). The chemical and pharmaceutical industries produce more than half of all hazardous waste. Other contributions are from garages, sheep dips, and the metals and metal products industries. Households account for only 3% of hazardous waste. Between 1984 and 1998, annual hazardous waste generation *almost tripled*, although this increase is partly a function of changes in definition. It is estimated that 20% of hazardous waste is *not reported*. In 1998, about 52% of reported hazardous waste was recovered – mainly solvents, organic substances and oil. The remaining 48% was disposed of, mainly through incineration and landfilling. Around 59% of reported hazardous waste was treated in Ireland (45% on-site and 14% off-site); 34% was exported, mainly to EU countries; and the remaining 7% was treated at an unspecified location.

2.   Responses

Objectives

General objectives regarding waste management were included in Ireland's 1990 Environment Action Programme (EAP). The EAP requested each local authority to prepare a waste recycling scheme, advocated construction of a central hazardous waste incinerator, and promoted packaging minimisation and use of biodegradable packaging. It also requested local authorities to strengthen clean-up activities.

The *1994 Recycling Strategy* introduced the principle of producer responsibility and set the following targets for 1999:

- an increase in municipal waste recycling from 7% (in 1993) to 20%: recycling of packaging waste (133 000 tonnes), diversion/composting of organic waste (110 000 tonnes), recycling/reuse of newsprint (15 000 tonnes) and other non-packaging waste (82 000 tonnes of paper, metals and textiles);

- expansion of the number of collection points for recyclable materials from 200 (mainly for glass) to 500 (multi-material), including some 20 civic amenity sites receiving segregated waste from the public (with 75 such sites planned in the longer term);

- recycling of 25% of metal, paper and plastic and 55% of glass, leading to an overall recycling rate of 33% by weight of packaging waste (compared with a 2001 target of 25% in the 1994 EU Packaging Directive).

The *1998 Policy Statement on Waste Management* sets the following targets for 2013:

- diversion of 50% of total household waste away from landfill;

- reduction of biodegradable waste consigned to landfill by a minimum of 65%;

- recycling of 35% of municipal solid waste;

- development of composting and other biological treatment facilities to handle 300 000 tonnes of organic waste annually;

- reduction of methane emissions from landfill by 80%;

- recovery of at least 85% of construction and demolition waste (at least 50% by 2003); and

- reduction of the number of municipal landfills from 75 to about 20, incorporating energy recovery and high environmental protection standards.

Institutional and regulatory framework

Only recently has waste management been the subject of separate legislation. Traditionally, it was perceived as part of the *public heath* functions of local authorities. The *1996 Waste Management Act* provides a comprehensive framework. Various waste management regulations have been issued subsequently. Under the Act:

- the EPA is responsible for integrated licensing of all significant waste disposal and recovery activities, including local authorities' landfills; planning hazardous waste management; authorising waste imports; monitoring and reporting on waste production and disposal; and monitoring and controlling licensed waste activities;

- major local authorities (county and city levels) have the responsibility of planning for non-hazardous waste management; authorising and controlling commercial waste collection activities; authorising waste exports and monitoring internal movements of hazardous wastes; permitting small-scale waste disposal and recovery activities; ensuring adequate collection and disposal arrangements for household waste; enforcing provisions of the Waste Management Act; and monitoring and inspecting waste activities in general;

- the Minister for the Environment and Local Government is empowered to issue policy directions to the EPA and local authorities regarding key aspects of waste management, and to prepare secondary legislation (Regulations).

The *1992 Environmental Protection Agency Act* provides an integrated pollution control (IPC) system which addresses waste generation, recovery and disposal and emphasises progressive waste minimisation at larger installations. The *1997 Litter Pollution Act* (which supersedes the 1982 Litter Act) identifies the various powers given to local authorities. It is an offence to litter in a public or visible place and while carrying on a business, as well as to present refuse for collection in a manner that creates litter. Controls on storage and disposal of radioactive waste are provided in the 1991 Radiological Protection Act.

Waste minimisation and disposal

Waste disposal

Most non-hazardous waste produced in Ireland (over 90% of municipal waste and more than two-thirds of industrial waste) goes to public or private *landfill* (Table 4.2). Only 60% of 95 communal landfills were monitored in 1995/96; 19% were assessed for groundwater quality, 12% for gas collection and 3% for presence of organic pollutants in leachate. A 1997 survey of 27 communal landfills identified problems common to many sites: lack of daily soil cover, inadequate

Table 4.2 **Waste disposal and recovery routes,** 1998[a]

(%)

Waste	Disposal					Recovery	Total
	Landfill	Incineration	Dumping at sea	Biological or chemical treatment	Other		
Commercial	91					9	100
Household	97					3	100
Industrial non-hazardous	66				4	30	100
Hazardous							
In Ireland	18	10		7	4	61	100
Exported	2	48				50	100
Municipal sludge	15		72		7	6	100
Dredge spoils			95			5	100
Total	66	–	7	–	3	24	100

a) Excluding agricultural waste and unreported hazardous waste.
Source: EPA.

leachate management, lack of surface water control or of litter control, poor waste compaction and untidy reception areas. While significant improvements are needed at many sites, some already operate to high standards. For example, the landfill at Kill (County Kildare), operating since 1997, has a capacity of over 6 million tonnes and applies the highest standards.

The *number of municipal landfills* fell from 95 in 1995 to 76 in 1998. Many are nearing capacity: 50% have a remaining lifespan of less than five years and 75% less than ten years. About 13% of active landfills are located on regional aquifers. Some of the closures are indicative of the trend towards fewer but larger engineered landfills. However, the majority of the 126 landfills reported in 1998 (76 municipal and 50 private/industrial) remain relatively small; 58% receive less than 15 000 tonnes per year and only 16% receive over 50 000 tonnes. There are 44 transfer stations, half in the Dublin region, where waste is compacted before it goes to disposal or recovery facilities.

Licensing obligations in respect of waste facilities, imposed on a phased basis since 1997, have applied to all facilities since October 1999. By the end of 1999, the EPA had received 136 waste licence applications, including 71 applications for landfills and 32 for transfer stations; 20 licenses and nine proposed decisions had been granted. There is considerable public interest in the waste licensing process. The EPA has received around 7 500 submissions to date.

There is not yet a *municipal waste incinerator* in Ireland. Incineration would facilitate meeting municipal waste recovery targets, which improved from 7.4% in 1993 to 9% in 1998 (compared with the 2013 target of 35%). The waste management plans being prepared at the regional level identify a need for *new waste treatment and disposal facilities*, including thermal treatment. Starting thermal treatment is envisaged only after new or upgraded waste reduction and recycling facilities are in place, probably not before 2004.

Waste minimisation: recycling and prevention

Waste recycling infrastructure consists of a combination of bring schemes in towns, one collect scheme in the Dublin region and individual bring banks, mostly in rural areas. *Bring schemes* are found principally in Counties Wicklow and Wexford. Most are privately owned. An exception is the most significant district recycler (Greystones in Wicklow), which provides one bring centre per 1 000 inhabitants. The principal operator is Rehab Recycling Partnership, in co-operation with local authorities. The materials brought by the public are glass, aluminium, cans, paper and textiles. The Dublin *collect scheme* was established in 1991. It was operated in 1999 by Kerbside Dublin, under a unique partnership including the Dublin Chamber of Commerce, industry, local authorities, the European Recovery and

Recycling Association (ERRA) and government bodies. Kerbside Dublin was replaced in 2000 by a more comprehensive household collection service, which will extend to 80% of homes in the Dublin region. Glass, paper, plastics and cans are collected weekly. In addition, there are 30 sites (mostly at landfills) where the public may deposit recyclable wastes.

Producer responsibility obligations were imposed by the 1997 Packaging Regulations. Major *packaging producers* must either comply with these Regulations or participate in an approved waste recovery scheme. One such scheme (Repak Ltd) was established in 1996 by industry in a voluntary agreement with government. Participants are required to take steps to recover their own packaging waste and must also contribute a participation fee. Repak supported recycling of 93 000 tonnes of packaging waste, or 13% of the total amount of this type of waste, in 1998. There is a target of 27% by 2001. Repak's total expenditure increased from IEP 1.5 million in 1998 to IEP 5.2 million in 1999. Repak introduced the pan-European "Green Dot" system in 1999. Licensing the Green Dot's use on packaged products has been proposed. The Irish Farm Films Producers Group has developed a similar recovery scheme for farm plastics such as sheeting, bale wrap, and bags for conserving fodder. In 1999, 4 100 tonnes of farm plastics was recycled through this scheme.

Most *construction and demolition waste* is removed to the cheapest available location, as strong competition in the construction sector does not allow waste segregation. In 1998, 43% of the construction and demolition waste sent to landfill was recovered. To meet the objectives of the 1998 Policy Statement on Waste Management, the construction industry established a task force to co-ordinate development of a voluntary recovery scheme for construction and demolition waste by 2000. The *automobile industry* has been invited to develop proposals for end-of-life vehicles and used tyres. The majority of end-of-life vehicles collected in Ireland are brought to two shredding plants at Cork and Dublin. There are no facilities or schemes for disposal of used tyres. In the case of car batteries, most of which are imported, no statutory producer responsibility obligation exists in regard to recycling. However, any facility for recovery of used batteries would be subject to EPA waste licensing or local authority permitting. Private companies have started to promote recycling of used lead-acid batteries; specially designed containers are delivered to collection sites such as garages, car dealers and local authorities, and a regular collection service is provided. DOELG is preparing a Policy Statement on Waste Recovery and Recycling, which will outline the scope of further *producer responsibility obligations*.

Progress in regard to *other waste streams* has been mixed. For *waste oil*, local authorities usually provide recycling banks at stand-alone and civic amenity centres. A number of recycling centres (such as those at Statoil garages) also provide oil collection facilities. Two private companies collect waste oil from the three major sources: garages, ships and industrial tank cleaning. In the case of *livestock slurries*, the sole disposal route is land spreading, which may lead to nitrate and phosphorus contamination of surface and groundwater. Provisions for nutrient management planning are included in the Local Government (Water Pollution) Act, and incentives to implement such plans are offered to farmers as part of the Rural Environmental Protection Scheme (Chapter 3). In the late 1990s, a significant share of *sewage sludge* from waste water treatment plants was landfilled (15%) or dumped at sea (72%). To prevent these practices, it was recently decided that local authorities should establish sludge management plans (Chapter 2). Disposal at sea was prohibited in 1999 (Chapter 7).

A discussion document on the potential to reduce industry's environmental impact through applying new *cleaner technologies* was published by DOELG in 1993. This document, "Cleaner Manufacturing Technologies in Ireland", identified the cleaner technologies most applicable for rapid uptake in Ireland and the major obstacles to their introduction. It proposed a programme of activity and measures to promote these technologies' development. The Operational Programme for Environmental Services 1994-99 supported a cleaner production pilot project in 14 companies, which gave rise to significant cost saving and waste minimisation. Both the EPA's Integrated Pollution Control system and IPC licensing, and the definition of BATNEEC for industrial sectors, favour cleaner technology and production improvements that prevent or minimise pollution.

Instruments and financing

In 1999, most local authorities published draft *waste management plans* (WMP) in compliance with the 1996 Waste Management Act and the 1997 Waste Management (Planning) Regulations. These statutory plans are in the process of being completed. Local authorities were encouraged to carry out preliminary strategy studies to evaluate available options and to adopt a regional approach to the planning process (eight waste management regions have been identified), with a view to increasing the efficiency of service provision. In some cases (such as in the Dublin region) a single regional plan was issued; in others, separate but inter-related plans were issued for each county/corporation within a region. The emphasis of WMP is on reducing reliance on landfills through implementing integrated waste management. The role of landfilling is changing to accommodate residual waste, following separation and recycling and (as appropriate) thermal treatment.

Capital investment in solid waste services was traditionally funded from *local authorities'* own resources. Operating costs were covered by "domestic rates" (local property taxes) until the 1978 abolition of these taxes on households. The revenue shortfall has since been made up out of a Rates Support Grant from the *central government.* In 1983, local authorities were empowered to levy *waste charges* to help meet the rising costs of supplying waste management services. Each authority is free to set its own charges.

Volume-related *waste charges* are widely applied to commercial users, though the level varies from one authority to another (Table 4.3). Of those local authorities providing household waste collection services in 2000, 19% (11 authorities) were not levying charges for this service, including three of the four authorities in the Dublin region. Where charges are levied on households, this is predominantly through flat rates. Charges are levied in all cases for direct disposal at landfill sites (gate fees). The majority of industrial waste is dealt with on-site and thus not directly affected by the charging system. The Waste Management Act allows local authorities to arrange for infrastructure provision and operation on a contract basis. Examples are the waste baling station at Ballymount (South Dublin County) and the landfill at Kill (County Kildare), both operated by the private sector.

Cost recovery for municipal waste *collection and disposal services* increased from 23% in 1994 to 51% in 1999 (Table 4.4). The remainder is financed by local authorities' general budgets and central government subsidies, which are also used for a number of household waste recycling projects. The EU-funded Operational Programme for Environmental Services 1994-99 includes a Waste Management Sub-Programme for improving waste management infrastructure and systems, under which investment of IEP 30.5 million has taken place in order to develop waste

Table 4.3 **Use of charges for waste collection and disposal,** 1994

Charge system	Household waste (% of population)	Commercial waste (number of local authorities)	Direct disposal of commercial waste to local authority landfill (number of local authorities)
No charge	40	2	2
Fixed charge	27	3	
Volume-related	18	10	17
Privatised collection	15	8	1[a]
No landfill in the area			3
Total	100	23[b]	23[b]

a) Privatised landfill.
b) Total number of survey respondents.
Source: ESRI.

strategies at local authority and regional level, improve (public and private) waste recycling infrastructure and support provision of hazardous waste infrastructure. The Local Government Fund established in 1999 provides local authorities with increased central government resources, part of which will be allocated to waste management.

Projected waste infrastructure over the period 2000-05 will require capital investment in the order of IEP 650-700 million. It is anticipated that 70% of this investment will come from the private sector (through public-private partnership arrangements), 15% from local authorities' own resources, and the remaining 15% from national and EU funding, which could include support for innovative technologies.

Hazardous waste management

Grant aid has been used to assist the provision and improvement of many *recovery and disposal* facilities. The overall environmental effectiveness of existing facilities is difficult to assess. Over 15 hazardous waste treatment facilities are in use, for which the EPA has received 14 waste licence applications. Irish industry has the capacity to incinerate 30% of total hazardous waste destined for incineration. Six hazardous waste incinerators are owned by big companies, and

Table 4.4   **Municipal waste management: operating expenditure and revenues**
(IEP million)

Expenditure	1994	1997	1998	1999[a]	1994	1997	1998	1999[a]	Revenues
Landfill operation	13	21	28	39	2	7	17	25	Landfill gate fees
Household collection	29	31	34	38	5	7	15	17	Household waste
Street cleaning	15	18	21	25	7	9	6	5	Commercial waste
Provision of landfills	1	3	5	4	1	6	12	17	Other
Commercial waste	0.5	1	1	1					
Litter prevention	0.5	1	1	1					
Loan charges	2	2	4	8					
Administration	4	5	7	8					
Total	65	82	101	124	15	29	50	64	Total
Cost recovery	23	35	49	51					

a) Estimate.
Source: DOELG.

three provide energy recovery. Overall, adequate treatment capacity exists for a number of waste streams; however, there are certain waste streams for which no processing capability exists.

Significant quantities of *hazardous waste are exported for recovery and disposal abroad*. Hazardous waste *exports* amounted to 100 000 out of a total 370 000 tonnes in 1998. In line with the proximity principle, Ireland strives for self-sufficiency in hazardous waste management. For example, as the stringent incineration plant emission levels required by EU legislation resulted in the closure of a number of hospital incinerators, a significant quantity of *hospital waste* was exported for safe disposal. Following the UK's import ban on hazardous hospital waste in 1998, however, a Joint Waste Management Board representing the Departments of Health in Northern Ireland and the Republic of Ireland was created. The Board appointed a contractor to provide a service to collect, treat and dispose of all healthcare risk waste throughout the island at three new facilities.

Ireland ratified the *Basel Convention* on the Control of Transboundary Movements of Hazardous Wastes and their Disposal in 1994. Since 1994, it has applied the 1993 EU Council Regulation on the supervision and control of shipments of waste within, into and out of the European Community. It thereby conforms to the OECD Council Decision on Transfrontier Movements of Wastes Destined for Recovery Operations and, in particular, has introduced a "green list" of wastes allowed to move subject only to controls normally applied in commercial transactions. The ban on exports to non-OECD countries has had no impact, as Ireland does not export hazardous waste outside the OECD area.

The EPA published a draft *National Hazardous Waste Management Plan* in 1999 for public consultation. The draft Plan has *prevention* as its primary focus. Although IPC licensing has resulted in the prevention of significant quantities of hazardous waste in industry, according to projections there is a need to achieve a 30% reduction in the generation of hazardous waste in 2006 just to remain at 1996 levels. The draft Plan recommends adopting a Prevention Programme aimed at ensuring there is no increase in the amount of hazardous waste subject to disposal.

Concerning hazardous waste *collection*, Ireland has a relatively well-developed waste brokerage industry. Its services have not generally been used by small businesses, commercial outlets, farms or households. Reasons include high unit cost, lack of awareness of waste management obligations and unwillingness to pay for hazardous waste disposal. The draft Plan recommends measures to ensure environmentally sound management of hazardous waste produced by such small generators. The EPA recently published a booklet, "Household Hazardous Waste", which explains how to manage and dispose of potentially harmful household products (e.g. cleaning agents, batteries, paints, pesticides, medicines).

3. Environmental Performance

As a result of economic growth, greater affluence and intensification of agriculture, an *increase in generation* of all types of waste (municipal, industrial, agricultural and hazardous) has occurred. Ireland has relatively *low waste recovery rates* and relies on *unsophisticated landfilling methods*. There is an urgent need to modernise waste management and to provide environmentally efficient infrastructure. *Public awareness and concern about waste disposal practices* is growing, and there is a consensus that waste needs to be managed in a planned and environmentally sound way. All this led in 1996 to *comprehensive new legislation on waste*, new policies for waste management (particularly recycling) and *investment in solid waste management* under the 1994-99 Operational Programme for Environmental Services.

Waste management planning was first introduced on a statutory basis in 1979 for non-hazardous and in 1982 for hazardous waste. Plans prepared by local authorities were mainly aimed at ensuring that adequate arrangements were made for safe waste disposal. No public consultation was required, and these plans did not have to address issues such as waste reduction or recovery. The 1996 Waste Management Act introduced radical changes in waste planning, the thrust of which is towards minimisation (prevention and recovery) and safe disposal of non-recoverable waste. The public must be consulted during the development of a plan. Local authorities are responsible for preparing waste management plans for all non-hazardous waste produced in their area, including agricultural waste and sludges. Most local authorities have jointly prepared regional waste management plans.

Waste disposal

Waste management infrastructure has been under-resourced, and significant capital investment will be needed to achieve the radical improvements called for. Over 90% of municipal waste is landfilled (Figure 4.2). More than 1 million tonnes of waste collected from households goes to *substandard landfill*. The 1999 EU Landfill Directive, which must be enacted in Irish law within two years, will impose strict environmental controls and standards relating to operation and aftercare. The waste collection network covers most of the country: only a small share of the *rural population is not yet served* on an organised basis.

Ireland is the only EU Member State *without incineration capacity* for municipal waste. A solution to the problem of *sewage sludge* disposal needs to be found rapidly, especially since volumes are likely to increase with the expansion of waste water treatment plants" capacity that is expected in the near future.

Waste prevention and recovery

Irish waste policy seeks to reflect the primacy given by EU legislation to waste prevention, reduction and re-use. The emphasis on *waste prevention and reduction* in the 1992 Environmental Protection Agency Act was reinforced in the 1996 Waste Management Act. A number of measures for promoting cleaner technologies have been implemented, including the establishment of a Clean Technology Centre at Cork Regional Technical College and a Cleaner Production Unit at the University College of Cork. Efforts to increase separate collection of municipal waste should be pursued. Collection rates for end-of-life vehicles and used tyres and batteries need to be improved.

By international standards, *waste recycling* rates in Ireland are very low. Progress was made between 1993 and 1998, when the overall recycling rate for packaging waste increased from 10 to 15%, but this is still far below target (Table 4.5). Substantial improvements can be made in the rate of recovery of materials from both household and commercial waste. The rate of recovery in industry is also low (30% for non-hazardous waste, 52% for hazardous). Over 85% of non-hazardous packaging waste produced in Ireland goes to public or private landfill. The 1997 Waste Management (Packaging) Regulations require suppliers of packaging either to participate in an approved waste recovery scheme or to implement steps themselves, including providing for return, recycling or segregation. The only approved body at present is Repak Ltd, whose packaging waste recovery scheme is open to all packaging suppliers. Meeting packaging waste

Table 4.5 **Recycling rates for packaging waste**
(%)

Waste	1993	1995	1998	Target 1999	Target 2005[a]
Paper	14	21	15	25	25-45
Plastic	0	0	3	25	25-45
Textile	0	0	0	25	25-45
Glass	21	32	32	55	25-45
Aluminium	4	13	4	25	25-45
Ferrous metals	0	2	4	25	25-45
Overall rate	10	16	15	33	50-65

a) In compliance with the 1994 EU Packaging Directive.
Source: EPA.

recycling targets would result in about 8% of municipal waste being diverted from landfill.

Local authorities and other public bodies have an important role to play in minimising the amount of *construction and demolition waste* being discarded. This can be achieved through measures such as co-ordinating service providers (water, gas, sewer) to avoid repeated excavations; ensuring that contracts require wastes to be segregated on-site and stored so as to facilitate recycling; developing specifications for construction materials that encourage recycling; and introducing charges that discourage disposal to landfill. Construction and demolition waste, though large in volume, is relatively easy to recycle and a market already exists for much of this material.

A considerable proportion of municipal solid waste consists of *organic materials that can be composted*. Composting (by households or at larger-scale centralised locations) should be encouraged as an alternative to disposal. In 1998, only 5 700 tonnes out of nearly 1.2 million tonnes of biodegradable municipal waste was reported as composted. A number of schemes are being implemented in Ireland. Centralised facilities are to be installed in several counties: each of the regional waste management plans provides for the development of centralised biological treatment facilities.

Instruments and financing

Many households pay relatively *low waste charges or none at all*, while charges levied on commercial generators are often well below the true cost of managing their waste. In 1998, local authorities spent nearly IEP 100 million on waste collection and disposal, but received a total income of some IEP 50 million from landfill gate fees and waste charges. Some authorities have adopted a tax system relating, to some extent, to the quantity of waste produced; bag-tagging and other use-related schemes are involved. However, most authorities levy flat-rate waste charges. In a Cork pilot project, waste charges are calculated according to the weight of the waste presented for collection. Deposit-refund schemes apply to farm plastics and, on an isolated and small-scale basis, to cans and plastic bags.

There is considerable scope for *increased private sector participation and investment in waste management* on a commercial basis. This is especially important with regard to the increased costs of meeting environmental standards relating to the licensing of waste disposal activities being applied by the EPA. There is a need to move towards full cost recovery for waste services. As a matter of equity, and to directly encourage waste reduction, weight-related charges should be introduced to the extent possible. Greater efforts should also be made to ensure that landfill gate fees correspond to the quantity of waste accepted for disposal. However, most Irish landfill sites do not have weigh-bridges, and high gate fees could lead to fly tipping. A complement to proper landfill pricing would be to introduce a landfill tax (per tonne) payable by landfill operators. This would ensure that landfill waste disposal is properly priced and would influence behaviour away from landfill towards re-use, recovery or recycling. For example, introduction of such a landfill tax in the UK in 1996 led to a drop in construction and demolition waste disposed to landfills.

Creation of *new capacity for composting, recycling and recovery* is being encouraged through DOELG grants intended to support capital investment in recycling facilities. The cost-effectiveness of these grants needs to be assessed. There is a role for public/private partnership in *developing markets for recyclables*, and in establishing and operating waste recovery and recycling facilities.

Hazardous waste management

Some 59% of reported *hazardous waste* generated nationally in 1998 was managed in Ireland, primarily through recovery/recycling (61%), landfilling (18%) and incineration (10%). There is no public or commercial hazardous waste incinerator. A draft National Hazardous Waste Management Plan was published by the EPA for public consultation. The aim of this Plan is to restrict hazardous waste generation to 1996 levels. A national hazardous waste prevention programme is at the heart of the Plan, with spending over seven years estimated at IEP 38 million. The draft Plan recommends that Ireland strive for self-sufficiency in hazardous waste management. It identifies two principal infrastructural gaps: hazardous waste landfill and thermal treatment capacity. Regional treatment centres will be established to treat hazardous hospital waste. Ireland has ratified the *Basel Convention* on the Control of Transboundary Movements of Hazardous Wastes and their Disposal. It also conforms to the OECD Council Decision on Transfrontier Movements of Wastes Destined for Recovery Operations.

Part II

INTEGRATION OF POLICIES

5

ENVIRONMENTAL AND ECONOMIC POLICIES

1. Towards Sustainable Development

The new Irish economy and environmental trends

Very rapid growth and dematerialisation

In the 1990s, the performance of the Irish economy (the "Celtic Tiger") was particularly impressive. Irish GDP per capita in 1990 was 74% of the EU average, but it is now well above the EU average and higher than that of the large European countries (Annex II). GNP per capita is, however, significantly lower, at 80% of the EU average. Since 1994, annual growth of GDP has been close to 9%, making the Irish economy *the fastest growing in the OECD*. Ireland's economic performance must also be assessed according to *other criteria*: budget surplus (+2.4%), positive trade balance (USD 18 billion), low inflation (2%), reduced unemployment (6%), but still significant poverty (low UNDP index). Exports represent 82% of Irish GDP (Chapter 1). *EU yearly net transfers* (representing 3-4% of GDP) and *foreign direct investment* (1 200 newly established overseas companies, annual transfers of USD 1.1 billion in the 1990s) have contributed to this performance.

In the 1990s, *industrial output grew* at an average of 14% annually (Table 5.1). Booming sectors of the new economy (e.g. electronics, pharmaceuticals) have *low energy and material intensity*. Energy intensity as a whole has therefore declined markedly. The number of foreign tourists per year increased from 3.1 million in 1990 to over 5.5 million, with Ireland's green image attracting a significant proportion. Greater affluence and demographic changes are responsible for rising consumption, and for changing consumption patterns.

Table 5.1   **Change in GDP, sectoral trends and environmental pressures**
(%)

	1980-98	1990-98
Selected economic trends		
GDP[a]	131.9	62.5
Population	8.9	5.8
GDP[a]/capita	112.9	53.6
Agricultural production	23.9	7.4
Industrial production[b]	321.1	128.2
Total primary energy supply	56.2	26.6
Energy intensity (per GDP)	−32.7	−22.1
Total final consumption of energy	50.3	28.8
Road traffic[c]	62.4	24.2
Selected environmental pressures		
CO_2 emissions from energy use[d]	46.2	19.0
SO_x emissions	−18.8	1.5
NO_x emissions	51.7	6.2
Municipal waste	221.4	36.4
Nitrogenous fertiliser use	43.6[e]	6.8[e]
Phosphate fertiliser use	−11.5[e]	−7.6[e]
Pesticide use	58.2[e]	33.2[e]

a) At 1991 prices and PPPs.
b) Includes mining and quarrying, manufacturing, gas, electricity and water.
c) Based on values expressed in vehicle-kilometres.
d) Excluding marine bunkers.
e) To 1997.
Source: OECD.

Changing consumption patterns

Improved income levels tend to be reflected not only in *consumption growth*, but also in *changing consumption patterns*: fast-growing demand for cars results in increased traffic, and growth in housing demand and urban sprawl in increased waste generation. These trends are reinforced by *demographic changes*: there has been a strong increase in population (particularly of young adults), along with declining average household size and continuing rural-to-urban migration.

Car ownership increased by almost 50% during the 1990s, and *car use* (vehicle-kilometres per capita) by almost 60%, generating urban air pollution, congestion and noise, particularly in urban and suburban areas, as well as stimulating demand for road infrastructure.

Over one-third of the Irish population lives in the *Greater Dublin Area* and approximately 80% lives in the 15 *coastal counties*. Irish *housing stock* is undergoing major changes, with related environmental infrastructure and service needs (e.g. water supply, waste water collection and treatment) and energy demands (e.g. for electricity). The housing market has *grown rapidly*: house building has more than doubled since 1993; the number of dwellings per 1 000 inhabitants increased from 244 in 1991 to 318 in 1998; and the demand will continue to be high in years to come. *House prices* have risen sharply, by about 60% for new and about 100% for second-hand houses since 1994, particularly in the Dublin area. Much of this growth is occurring in suburbs, accompanied by *urban sprawl*. The new Planning and Development Bill is designed to improve the spatial planning context (i.e. strategic planning, development planning, coastal management) in which much of this change is occurring.

Environmental trends

During the 1990s, SO_x, NO_x and CO_2 *emissions* were stabilised or continued to increase, although at a lower rate than GDP. SO_x emission intensities per unit of GDP are still above the OECD average, and reductions have been less than in most other OECD countries. NO_x and CO_2 emissions per unit of GDP are similar to or above OECD Europe averages. While industry managed to reduce CO_2 emissions by 20% compared with 1980, despite a 321% increase in production, emissions from transport and energy transformation grew by about 65 and 75%, respectively.

Municipal waste generation has increased rapidly, doubling over the last 15 years as a result of population growth and increased per capita waste generation.

Commercial fertiliser use has shown little change, but commercial fertilisers are only part of the nutrient balance. The major input is provided by organic nutrients from livestock. Since the early 1980s, the number of poultry has increased by 35%, that of pigs by 73% and that of sheep by 142%. The *total organic load* generated by agricultural activity in Ireland is equivalent to that of about 68 million people. Intensification and concentration of agricultural production has led to increased eutrophication, greenhouse gas emissions and, in some parts of the country, overgrazing.

Institutional integration of environmental concerns

Investment programming in the EU context

Ireland's relationship with the European Union influences Irish environmental policies primarily through EU directives and funding. As mentioned earlier, EU net funding transfers have reached 3-4% of GDP: roughly one-half through the Common Agricultural Policy (CAP) and the other half through the Cohesion Policy. In particular, Cohesion Policy investments under the Structural Funds have been made through *Community Support Frameworks* (CSFs) and the two related *National Development Plans*. While the first Irish CSF (1989-93) mentioned environmental issues only marginally, they gained importance in the second CSF (1994-99). This applies not only to the environmental measures of the Environmental Services Operational Programme, but also to other Operational Programmes (e.g. Rural Development OP, Energy Subprogramme of the Economic Infrastructure OP). In addition, funds from the EU *Cohesion Fund* are increasingly devoted to environmental investment projects (almost exclusively related to water).

In response to obligations following the *EU Structural Fund Regulations*, mechanisms have been established to ensure better appraisal of environmental opportunities and impacts relevant to Structural Funds intervention. More generally, Irish efforts to better integrate environmental concerns in sectoral policies are related to the respective EU environmental policy initiatives, such as the *Fifth Environmental Action Programme* and the Commission Communications on Cohesion Policy and the Environment, as well as the Partnership for Integration endorsed by the Cardiff European Council.

The national Sustainable Development Strategy

The 1997 Sustainable Development Strategy for Ireland was the result of a *long process* beginning in 1990, with the approval of the first National Environment Action Programme. It also builds on the vision of the place of the environment in Ireland's economic and social development expressed by the GREEN 2000 Advisory Group, established in 1991. This cross-sectoral group emphasised that Irish employment was partly dependent on a clean and good quality environment, as well as on the country's green image. In 1995 a baseline review of environmental policy and developments, "Moving Towards Sustainability", was published.

The *overall aim* of the 1997 Sustainable Development Strategy is "to ensure that the economy and society in Ireland can develop to their full potential within a well-protected environment, without compromising the quality of that environment, and with responsibility towards present and future generations and the wider international community."

The strategy itself results from a process of interdepartmental co-operation and co-ordination in which various other stakeholders are also involved. It includes:

- an analysis of relationships between *economic activities and the environment*, and an agenda to reinforce and deepen institutional integration of environmental concerns;

– presentation of a wide range of objectives and measures defined in a series of *sectoral action programmes* (agriculture, forestry, marine resources, energy, industry, transport and tourism);

– a description of *accompanying measures*, in particular concerning physical and spatial planning, information and awareness, indicators, monitoring, and international co-operation on the environment.

Implementing the Sustainable Development Strategy: institutional arrangements

The *Environmental Network*, established in 1994, was relaunched in 1998 and has become an inter-ministerial committee at Assistant Secretary level. Its mandate is to ensure environmental integration through better co-ordination and consultation across Departments. The network is complemented by regular meetings of liaison or purchasing officers of Departments.

A *National Sustainable Development Partnership (Comhar)* was created in 1999 to serve as a representative forum for public-private consultation and dialogue on sustainable development issues. Members were nominated by five panels comprising bodies and organisations representative of the State, sector, economic sectors, environmental NGOs, social/community NGOs and the professional/academic sector. Fifty-nine organisations were invited to nominate the 25 members, who are appointed for three-year terms. Comhar is to provide independent advice to the Government, promote integration of environmental considerations in socio-economic activities, recommend innovative policy options and instruments, and contribute to enhancement of information exchange and public awareness concerning sustainable development throughout Irish society. It will also represent Ireland in relevant international consultative fora, including the UNCSD. Four working groups have been established, focusing on: i) policy mechanisms and instruments, such as environmental taxation, eco-labelling, voluntary agreements, eco-auditing of policies; ii) long-term strategic spatial planning, which is a medium-term priority; iii) waste prevention, minimisation, reuse and recycling; and iv) Local Agenda 21 themes, with an emphasis on education, participation and involvement.

Implementing the Sustainable Development Strategy: policy integration

Anticipating or responding to the 1997 Sustainable Development Strategy, several Departments have adopted *strategic sectoral policy documents* in areas such as tourism ("Developing Sustainable Tourism", 1994), forestry ("Growing for the Future", 1996), integrated coastal management (1997), health, heritage, agriculture and energy (all in 1998), and marine and natural resources ("Strategy Statement", 1998-2000).

In 1999 the Government approved the introduction, on a pilot basis, of a procedure for strategic *environmental assessment of sectoral policies.* Implementation of the new National Development Plan, which will form the basis for significantly reduced European Structural Fund interventions in the period 2000-06, is a unique opportunity to make progress in this field. These environmental assessments will, to the extent possible, quantify significant positive or negative environmental impacts, whether direct or indirect; consider alternative policy options; describe measures to eliminate or mitigate potentially harmful impacts; and provide for follow-up assessment. The results should be summarised in memoranda to the Government on policy proposals and become part of the explanatory memoranda to bills.

To strengthen national efforts to promote sustainable development, *Local Agenda 21* initiatives have been encouraged; by 1998, local authorities had been requested to prepare a Local Agenda 21 and to identify Agenda 21 officers. These officers are linked to a national network through regional representatives, providing a forum for exchange of experience and good practice examples.

Economic impacts of environmental policies

Environmental expenditure

In 1998, public and private environmental expenditure (defined as expenditure on pollution abatement and control, water supply and nature protection) is estimated to have been 1% of GDP. *PAC expenditure is estimated at 0.6% of GDP.* Water pollution, waste and air pollution related expenditure represented 62, 30 and 7% of total PAC expenditure, respectively.

In the late 1990s, water related expenditure (water supply, sewerage and sewage treatment) was evenly shared between capital investment and operating expenditure, while waste related expenditure was almost entirely for operating expenditure. The *large majority of investment concerned water supply and waste water collection and treatment;* very little concerned air pollution abatement and control and waste management.

Environmental expenditure increased during the 1990s, as a result of growth in water infrastructure investment and in water and waste related current expenditure. *Public environmental expenditure* (Table 5.2), representing 88% of total environmental expenditure, was mostly concerned with water and waste. Private expenditure is not well-documented and was mostly related to water and air.

Financing of environmental expenditure

Financing of environmental expenditure is dominated by *public funding.* This reflects i) a tradition of public financing of water and waste related services by taxpayers through public budgets, rather than by users through service related changes; and ii) EU financing of water infrastructure. Given the very centralised Irish fiscal system (Chapter 1), this gives a major funding role to DOELG. Limited use is made of the Polluter-Pays and User-Pays Principles.

Between 1994 and 1999, *financing* of environmental (mostly water related) infrastructure was largely supported (i.e. up to 70%) by *EU Cohesion and Structural Funds*. The overall *Irish effort* in 1998 is estimated at *0.5% of GDP for PAC expenditure* and *0.8% of GDP for environmental expenditure*. This is low compared to most other OECD countries.

Competitiveness

There is no evidence that environmental measures and expenditure in Ireland have adversely affected economic growth or *international competitiveness*. On the contrary, the country's green image has been cultivated and is perceived as an asset with regard to the tourism industry. The large influx of foreign direct

Table 5.2 **Public environmental expenditure**

(IEP million)

	1994	1998	1999[a]
Central budget	**119**	**197**	**302**
of which: Investment expenditure			
Water	110	183	276
Waste	1	2	7
Operating expenditure			
EPA	5	8	9
Other env. services	3[b]	4	11
Local authorities	**223**	**297**	**341**
of which: Operating expenditure			
Water	138	170	189
Waste	66	102	124
Other env. services	19	26	28
Total public expenditure	**342**	**494**	**643**
of which: Investment expenditure	111	185	283
Operating expenditure	231	309	360

a) Anticipated expenditure.
b) Estimated figure.
Source: DOELG; OECD.

investment and the export orientation of much of the new economy have helped induce relevant enterprises to closely follow EMAS or ISO 14000 standards.

2. Environmental Policy Instruments

Regulatory instruments

Irish environmental legislation (Table 1.1) has developed over the years, including recently with the enactment of the 1996 Waste Management Act. The 1992 *Environmental Protection Agency Act* marked a major change in national environmental policy. Since Ireland joined the EU in 1973, EU environmental legislation has had a key influence on its environmental law (Chapter 7).

Licensing

Before 1992, local authorities had the primary responsibility for environmental protection. The 1992 Environmental Protection Agency Act established a new pollution control body, the *Environmental Protection Agency* (EPA), with, inter alia, licensing, monitoring and enforcement responsibilities. It also established *Integrated Pollution Control (IPC)*, requiring integrated permits for medium to large industries covering air, water, noise and waste/soil. Local authorities still grant single medium permits for small installations (e.g. in the dairy industry) under various acts. The EPA has a general supervisory role in relation to the performance by local authorities of their environmental protection functions.

IPC licenses are based on application of *BATNEEC* (best available technology not entailing excessive costs), with an emphasis on pollution prevention techniques including cleaner technologies and waste minimisation. Guidance on what constitutes best available technology is given by the EPA. The license includes conditions to ensure that the operator employs BATNEEC, and that the activity will not result in significant environmental pollution. It is expected that there will be 700-800 activities requiring permitting. Of these, some 470 have already submitted applications; about 300 licenses have been issued since 1994, when permitting commenced. By 2002, full licensing is expected to have taken place. Until IPC licensing is required for a category of activity, it remains under local authority control for single-medium licences. Licences are to be reviewed every five to ten years. The EPA may review them after three years. IPC licenses are based on information from companies themselves and from EPA monitoring.

The *application fee* the EPA charges for IPC licenses is specified for each sector, depending on the complexity of the permitting process. An *annual fee* covers the costs of compliance monitoring. The EPA is responsible for all aspects of permitting, inspection and enforcement. IPC licenses are issued only by the EPA.

The EPA operates a comprehensive database covering all aspects of permitting and enforcement. A condition for granting an IPC license is that the operator shall "establish and maintain" an *Environmental Management System (EMS)*. This is not necessarily a formalised EMS system (such as EMAS or ISO 14000), but a review of all operations and of practicable options for implementing cleaner technology, cleaner production and waste reduction or minimisation. The licensee is expected to provide on-site *public access to all files relating to environmental performance*. The EMS is audited as part of routine EPA inspection of a facility.

The EPA also provides advice and assistance to local authorities, and it exercises general *supervision over local authorities' environmental protection performance*. A specific management system, based on EMAS and ISO 14001, has been set up to carry out these responsibilities. It categorises the environmental responsibilities of local authorities as follows: water quality, waste water, miscellaneous, planning, noise, air and waste. This management system is intended to produce sector reports, which will in turn form a basis for national reports on how local authorities fulfil their environmental obligations. The EPA is presently undertaking a pilot of the system for three local authorities.

Compliance and enforcement

Concerning activities subject to IPC licensing, compliance assessment and enforcement are carried out by *EPA inspectors*. Assessments include on-site inspections, detailed audits, and review of data and reports submitted by operators. There was a substantial increase in site inspections and EPA monitoring visits to IPC sites during the second half of the 1990s (Table 5.3).

Self-monitoring, an important part of compliance assessment which is specified in the permit conditions, is carried out to check compliance with limit values for air pollution, waste, water effluent, groundwater, noise and odour. Self-monitoring programmes are designed by the inspector, depending on the nature and load of the pollutants emitted, the equipment required, the amount of information included in the permit application and its validity, the receiving media and the site history.

In cases of *non-compliance*, the EPA can take action against a company. For minor non-compliance, the licensee is notified and is directed to correct it. Where major non-compliance is determined, the licensee is directed to correct it within a specified period. Failure to take appropriate corrective actions within this period may lead to further enforcement action, such as a *section notice* under the Air or Water Pollution Acts or *prosecution* under the EPA Act (Table 5.3). In certain cases, the EPA has required immediate work to be carried out to avoid continuing pollution.

The *sanctions* under the various regulations are: maximum fine, IEP 10 000 000 and/or ten years imprisonment (EPA Act); maximum fine, IEP 25 000 and/or five years imprisonment (Water Pollution Act); maximum fine, IEP 20 000 and/or two years imprisonment (Air Pollution Act). In 1997, the EPA launched seven prosecutions against non-compliant facilities, all of which were successful. Fines were marginal, however, ranging from IEP 450 to 1 050 plus procedure costs. Local authorities can also undertake enforcement action. In 1997, under the Water Pollution Act, they carried out some 6 000 investigations and initiated 56 prosecutions.

Table 5.3   **Integrated pollution control: licensing, monitoring and enforcement**

	1994/95	1996	1997	1998
Number of applications	86	210	376	480
Monitoring visits by EPA staff to IPC sites	280	504	889	997
Site visits by EPA inspectors to IPC sites	–	350	550	744
Samples analysed by EPA laboratories	794	1 272	1 909	2 095
Audits	10	21	60	101
Enforcement notices	14	57	164	185
Prosecutions	0	4	7	7

Source: EPA.

Economic instruments

Ireland has made only *limited use of economic instruments* in environmental management so far (Table 5.4). While some funding is provided for incentive payments and remuneration of environmental services, particularly in the context of agricultural policy, charges are of marginal importance. To some extent, present practice and recent decisions are inconsistent with the intention to make polluters pay and to confront consumers of scarce resources with their actual costs.

However, pertinent research has been undertaken by the Economic and Social Research Institute (ESRI) and an *Interdepartmental Group on Environmental Taxation*, chaired by the Department of Finance, has been established. As part of the budgeting process, this Group is preparing short reports reviewing the current situation and presenting options for increased use of environmental taxes

Table 5.4 **Economic instruments**

Instruments	Details	Comments
Charges		
Water		
Domestic	Charges abolished in 1997, previously flat rate.	No metering.
Other	Volume-based for supply, less so for sewage.	
Waste		
Domestic	Mainly flat rate.	19% of local administrations do not charge.
Other	Mainly volume-based.	Cost recovery in 1994 25%, in 1998 50%.
Tax relief for car scrapping	IEP 1 000 relief if ten-year-old car is scrapped. Approx. 20% of VRT revenue.	Ran from July 1995 for two years. 60 000 cars (or 6% of stock) scrapped.
Subsidies		
Food industry	Pollution control grants.	8-10% of investment.
Industry and commerce		
Energy audit grant	40%, up to IEP 3 000, for audit.	IEP 2 million expenditure in first year, 1995.
Efficiency grant	Up to 40%, to IEP 156 000, for investment.	
Agriculture and rural development		
Rural Environment Protection Scheme (REPS)	Premium of IEP 122/ha, up to max. 40 ha. Extra for Natural Heritage Areas (NHAs), Special Protection Areas (SPAs), Special Areas of Conservation (SACs) and organic farming.	Part of 1992 CAP reform. Budget of IEP 460 million over several years.
Control of Farmyard Pollution Scheme (1994-99)	Grants up to 60%, to a value of IEP 13 500, to small farms for slurry storage, etc.	Under Operational Programme (OP) for Agriculture, Rural Development and Forestry.
Afforestation grant	IEP 1 300-3 000 per ha, plus 20-year premium of IEP 130-300 per ha.	Part of CAP reform. Also OP grants for forestry improvement and amenity.
Energy		
Compensation payments	On social grounds for use of alternative fuels to bituminous coal.	IEP 9 million expenditure per year.

Source: OECD.

and charges. In the 1999 Budget Statement, the Minister of Finance stated that "Tax increases on energy and fuels can reduce emissions and bring about more efficient use of these products. The revenue raised might also be used to reduce taxation in other areas such as labour." He proposed that the formulation of such policy measures be part of discussions on the successor to the "Partnership 2000" *agreement between the Government and its social partners.*

Charges

In 1997, exceptionally in the case of an OECD country, *water charges* for Irish private households were abolished. In 1994, recovery of the operating costs of environmental services delivered by local authorities had reached only 75% for water supply and 18% for waste water treatment. Since businesses are not exempt from water charges, significant distortions are built into the system (Table 5.4). *Lack of metering* in private dwellings is a major hurdle when it comes to applying pricing for water services. Newly constructed dwellings do not appear to be equipped with meters.

Again, in regard to *solid waste*, most Irish households are not expected to pay actual disposal costs. In 2000, about one-fifth of local authorities were not charging households at all; others were applying flat rates linked to property value. Recovery of operating costs has been improving, increasing from less than 25% in 1994 to almost 50% in 1998 (Table 5.4). Deposit-refund schemes are not well developed: to date, only a modest scheme is applied to cans on some of the islands. Some supermarkets offer an indirect refund, usually given to worthy causes and charities, for the return of plastic bags.

A *car scrappage scheme*, operating between 1995 and 1997, eliminated some of the oldest vehicles. It allowed IEP 1 000 of the vehicle registration tax payable on a new vehicle to be refunded if a car over ten years old was scrapped. Some 60 000 cars (about 6% of the stock) were scrapped under this scheme (Table 5.4).

Financial support

Financial support can take different forms, including *subsidies* (e.g. grants, low interest loans and tax allowances) or *direct payments* for provision of public goods and services. Subsidies are offered to firms that undertake environmental audits, or for training in environmental management and energy use in industry. In Dublin and Cork, where use of bituminous coal is banned, *compensation payments* are provided on social grounds to compensate for the additional cost of smokeless fuels (Table 5.4).

Environmentally targeted payments to agriculture include i) investment aid under the Control of Farmyard Pollution Scheme and the Farm Improvement Programme, ii) incentives for particular efforts to reduce pollution or degradation caused by farming activities, and iii) remuneration for maintaining or enhancing environmentally beneficial management practices (Table 5.4).

Environment related taxation and tax differentiation (energy and transport taxation)

Revenues from environment related taxes are higher than the OECD average, measured as a share of GDP and as a share of total tax revenues (Table 5.5). Ireland currently applies a reduced rate of 12.5% *value added tax (VAT)* to energy products including electricity. Most other EU countries apply the standard VAT rate to energy products. For Ireland this would imply an increase to 21% with significant implications for households and, to a lesser extent, for commercial enterprises, since they can deduct the VAT from taxes owed. No decision has been taken as yet, but these implications have been studied. One issue is the risk of distorted incentives in areas bordering Northern Ireland, since the United Kingdom's VAT rate on household energy use was reduced from 8 to 5% recently: a tax differential of 16 instead of 7.5 percentage points would provide undesired incentives for cross-border trading of coal and other fuels.

Fuel taxes comprise the VAT and an excise tax, with differing rates for petrol, diesel and LPG. For these products Ireland applies the EU minimum rates. Fuel tax increases have been moderate since 1990. The retail price of petrol, especially diesel, is now lower in Ireland than in the United Kingdom (including Northern Ireland). A lower excise tax has applied to unleaded petrol, compared to that on leaded and super unleaded. Leaded petrol represented over 90% of total sales in 1989 and less than 10% some ten years later. In compliance with EU legislation, it was removed from the market by the end of 1999.

To influence the balance between private and *public transport*, refunds on fuel used for the latter have been in effect since the mid 1970s (the refund is currently 93% of the tax on diesel). In 1996, the cost of these tax concessions was in the order of IEP 12 million. Since 1999, public transport has been encouraged by two additional tax measures: accelerated *capital allowances* are provided for construction of park and ride facilities in urban areas, with the aim of encouraging motorists to leave their cars outside the congested city centre and complete the journey by public transport; and *provision of bus and rail passes*, valid for one month or more, by employers to employees is no longer subject to income tax as a benefit in kind.

A *vehicle registration tax (VRT)* has been in effect since 1993. Payable on first registration of the vehicle in Ireland, it applies to new and second-hand cars coming from within or outside the EU. Rates are differentiated with respect to value and engine power. The VRT on private cars was reduced in 1994 and 1997. A three-tier VRT was introduced in 1999 to encourage purchase of smaller cars.

In 1993, gross VRT receipts were IEP 183 million; they had risen to IEP 462 million in 1998. Vehicles are also subject to a *motor vehicle tax* differentiated between private cars, goods vehicles, buses and other vehicles. The rate is lower for smaller engines and electric cars.

In 1998, tax relief was introduced as an incentive to corporate investment in *renewable energy*. To encourage and speed up private investment in pollution control facilities, special capital allowances were offered for a three-year period beginning in March 1999.

Table 5.5   **Environment related taxes,** 1999

Taxes	Rate	Comments
Fuel taxes	IEP 0.361/l (leaded petrol) IEP 0.357l (super unleaded petrol) IEP 0.294/l (unleaded petrol) IEP 0.256/l (diesel) IEP 0.181/l (aviation petrol) IEP 0.042/l (LPG) IEP 0.037/l (green diesel) IEP 0.025/l (kerosene) IEP 0.014/l (non-automotive LPG) IEP 0.011/l (heavy fuel oil)	– Exemptions: exports; internal commercial flights and external flights; sea navigation; vehicles for disabled persons; purposes other than use as motor or heating fuel; manufacture of alumina (heavy fuel oil). – 93% refund for diesel used in licensed passenger road services; for horticultural production, refund on green diesel (88%), LPG (69%) and heavy fuel oil (58%).
Motor vehicle tax	IEP 160-2 494/year (goods vehicles) IEP 98-849/year (private cars) IEP 78-206/year (buses) IEP 98/year (private electric cars) IEP 49/year (electric goods vehicles, school buses, taxis) IEP 22/year (motorcycles)	– Exemptions: public services (State-owned vehicles, local authorities, fire brigade vehicles, ambulances, road construction, street cleaning); diplomatic vehicles; vehicles for disabled persons. – Private cars: rate increases with motor engine capacity; Goods vehicles: rate increases with unladen weight; Buses: rate increases with number of seats.
Vehicle registration tax	22.5-30% of open market sales price, with minimum IEP 250/veh. (cat. A) 13.3% of open market sales price, with minimum IEP 100/veh. (cat. B) IEP 40/veh. (cat. C) IEP 2/cc (motorcycles)	– Exemptions: public services, diplomatic vehicles, category D vehicules. – Category A: rate increases with cylinder capacity; Motorcycles: reduced rate of IEP 1/cc above 350 cc, reduction for age.

Source: OECD.

Other instruments

Spatial planning

Land use planning in Ireland has existed far longer than have environmental controls. The 1963 Local Government (Planning and Development) Act established a comprehensive authorisation procedure for new development, including the requirement to consider environmental matters. Responsibility for *land use and spatial planning* rests primarily with local planning authorities under the general direction of DOELG. To limit traffic and halt the decline of urban centres, in 1998 DOELG instructed local authorities not to authorise supermarkets of over 3 000 square metres.

By the end of 1997, there were *local development plans* for 34 counties, five county boroughs, nine borough corporations and 49 urban districts. In the same year, 56 000 *planning permissions* were requested, of which 90% were granted. In the case of unauthorised development, or development that does not comply with a planning permission, local authorities must take appropriate action. At national level an appeals board (*An Bord Pleanála*) can act in case of conflicts. Its members represent different interests, such as planning, environmental protection and amenity preservation, economic development and construction, local government, and social interest groups.

By the end of the 1990s, no general national strategic document providing guidance for spatial development initiatives had been adopted. Only in 1999 had *strategic planning guidelines* been defined for the fast growing Greater Dublin Area. Following a commitment in the Government Programme "An Action Programme for the Millennium", a new *Planning and Development Bill* was presented in 1999. Consolidating and revising previous legislation, it introduces a more strategic and integrated approach to territorial development. In particular:

- *strategic planning guidelines at regional level* will provide a more strategic context for development plans. Statutory recognition is given to the Strategic Planning Guidelines for the Greater Dublin Area (1999), which will serve as a kind of reference for similar guidelines to be developed by other regional authorities;

- *sustainable development* will become a more explicit dimension of the planning process. There will be mandatory environmental protection objectives in development plans, and environmental assessment requirements for plans and planning guidelines;

- *environmental impact assessment (EIA)*, founded in primary legislation, will include provisions that go beyond the requirements of the EU's EIA Directive;

- new provisions governing the interface between *planning control and IPC licensing* will be introduced;
- provisions will be made for conservation of *amenities, landscape*, trees, architectural heritage, etc.

The Planning and Development Bill also aims at streamlining and speeding up the planning system, in order to minimise delays in housing, commercial and infrastructure development. In particular:

- third parties must express their objections to planning authorities before exercising their *right of appeal* to An Bord Pleanála;
- *fees* will be charged those parties submitting observations to planning authorities concerning planning applications;
- planning decisions will be taken within eight to 12 weeks.

Under the National Development Plan (2000-06) DOELG was mandated to prepare a National Spatial Strategy (NSS) by 2002, providing a framework for longer-term spatial development at the national level.

Environmental impact assessment (EIA)

The 1985 EU Directive on Environmental Impact Assessment was transposed into Irish law and made operational in 1990. EIA was required for projects listed in EU Annex I (mandatory) and, regardless of their size and location, for several project types listed in Annex II (e.g. mining and petroleum extraction, chemical and pharmaceutical production, fish meal and fish oil plants). Size thresholds were set for other Annex II project types. Subsequent amendments enlarged the scope of EIAs to include, for example, all projects subject to IPC licensing, and to transpose amendments introduced under EU Directive 97/11/EC. One notable feature of Irish EIA practice is that, while the system of *project size thresholds* is retained, special measures are adopted in environmentally sensitive areas to ensure that the need for assessment is examined regardless of project size. Furthermore, State Authorities must obtain planning permission in the same way as private sector developers.

The *EIA procedure* is integrated into the planning process and IPC licensing. Local authorities or the EPA, as appropriate, review the EIA's quality and consider its results. The public has access to studies and can present comments on the development application; authorities' decisions are published in the press. The new Planning and Development Bill foresees that initial development applications will contain an environmental impact statement (EIS). Planning authorities, and An Bord Pleanála on appeal, will consider the EIS when evaluating a development application. This could bring further improvement, provided the EIS is not too rudimentary.

Environmental research and development

Research and development can contribute significantly to the evolution of new and more efficient ways to protect and manage natural resources and the environment. Although Ireland's economic success partly reflects a strategic choice to focus on dynamic high-tech branches (electronics, pharmaceuticals, etc.), its *attitude to research and development* has long been relatively passive. Much innovation relies on foreign investors.

In the Tierney report (1995), part of a comprehensive review of *science, technology and innovation* in Ireland, concern was expressed that a properly funded and structured research programme to support environmental enterprises in Ireland did not exist. Although the Government announced in a White Paper on Science, Technology and Innovation (1996) that the 1997 Sustainable Development Strategy would take the relevant Tierney recommendations into account, the strategy touches only briefly on research and the potential benefits of science and technology.

Since it was established in 1994, the *EPA* has become an important promoter of *environmental research*. The EU Operational Programme for Environmental Services (1994-99) devoted about 3% of public expenditure to environmental R&D, focusing on environmentally sustainable resource management and cleaner production. Particular attention was to be given to ecosystem research, envirosocio-economic research, monitoring capability, waste reduction, promotion of cleaner manufacturing technologies and eco-auditing.

A *research centre for environmental policy* has been established in Dublin, in agreement with DOELG and the Economic and Social Research Institute (ESRI). Studies have been undertaken on waste management, sustainable development indicators, environmental effects of taxes and subsidies, and other subjects. The centre has contributed to the mid-term assessment of EU Structural Fund environmental interventions in Ireland.

Environmental information and education

Public access to environmental information is legally guaranteed by regulations issued in 1993, following the 1990 EU Directive on *Freedom of Access to Information* on the Environment. Access is also organised through specific arrangements established under the planning system and the IPC licensing mechanism. The EPA publishes State of the Environment reports at least once every five years; the most recent was published in 1996, and a new one is expected in 2000. The EPA register of all IPC licences is accessible to the public at the EPA headquarters. The EPA also circulates copies of applications, and details of decisions and actions, to the relevant planning authority for local public access.

In 1990, a national *environmental information centre (ENFO)* was set up to provide easy public access to wide-ranging and authoritative information on all aspects of the environment and sustainable development, and to foster increased environmental awareness. ENFO, which has an annual budget of IEP 400 000 and a staff of 12, is centrally located in Dublin, where it receives about 50 000 visitors annually. The reference library contains some 55 000 titles, including EIA texts and the IPC licences issued by EPA. A series of over 120 information leaflets on issues such as waste recycling and energy conservation, and a variety of brochures and documents published by DOELG, are available. Increasingly information is also made available on the ENFO website. A particular focus of ENFO activities is environmental education in schools.

Environmental education is also promoted through initiatives like the *Green Schools Programme*, launched by An Taisce in co-operation with local authorities, which addresses about 300 schools and provides training material for primary school teachers. A network of visitor centres in protected areas and parks distributes high quality environmental information.

Participation and partnership

Environmental NGOs play an important role in raising the environmental awareness of the general public, administrative authorities and enterprises. Participation is arranged under the Planning and Development Act, as well as under the IPC licensing mechanism. Environmental NGOs are actively engaged at the national level, for example in Comhar, the National Sustainable Development Partnership, and locally in Agenda 21 committees. Staff, resources and external support are limited. Covering a wide range of concerns, these NGOs are making efforts to provide quality input in the various environmental policy areas. A particular challenge is monitoring the environmental implications and impacts of the massive investments undertaken in the context of EU co-funded schemes.

An *Environmental Partnership Fund*, created in 1997 to support partnership agreements between local authorities, local community groups and environmental NGOs, provides small grants (usually in the order of IEP 2 000-4 000) for environmental awareness projects at the local level. In 1999, total funding was doubled to IEP 200 000. It was used to support six national and 65 local projects.

3. Environmental Performance

Ireland generally has *good environmental quality*. Thanks to its environmental policies and to the "*new economy*", energy and material intensities fell in the 1990s. However, despite progress in some areas, particularly with regard to reducing emissions and effluents from industry, a lessening of environmental pressures has not yet been achieved. *Pollution intensities are often high* compared to those in other European countries. Major problems remain concerning environmental pressures from energy production and agriculture, particularly intensive livestock rearing. Pressures relating to municipal waste water are gradually decreasing with investment in waste water treatment, but they remain high. There are growing problems associated with changes in *consumption patterns* (e.g. waste generation, transport and urban sprawl, particularly in the Dublin and Cork areas).

Integrating environmental concerns in economic decisions

During the 1990s, Ireland experienced i) steady economic growth (the highest among OECD countries); ii) structural change, with the rapid growth of, inter alia, information technology and biotechnology based industries; iii) improved income levels; iv) a growing population and suburbanisation, particularly in Dublin, Cork and other coastal areas. Tourism has expanded rapidly, building on the country's "green image". The emergence of a "new economy" has translated into a *decrease in the energy and material intensities of production* (per unit of GDP), but not an absolute decrease in environmental pressures. Overall, only a weak decoupling has taken place, compared to best international practices. Transition to the new economy has also translated into an *increase in environmental pressures relating to consumption*: greater waste generation, greater motorisation and mobility, greater land consumption, and related demands for environmental infrastructure.

Some *sectors and industries* that have serious negative impacts on the environment continue to benefit from low taxation and from subsidies, including EU support. For example, *peat based electricity production* is controversial given its low economic efficiency (as a subsidised activity) and environmental effects (air emissions, damage to landscapes and habitats); economic incentives with regard to *agriculture* should be reconsidered under the revised EU Common Agricultural Policy, to take advantage of "cross-compliance" opportunities (making farm support conditional on compliance with environmental standards) and agri-environmental payments (under the REPS programme). Overall, distortions created by subsidies for *energy and agricultural production* should be reduced and should contribute to increased environmental effectiveness and economic efficiency.

In 1997, Ireland issued a *national Sustainable Development Strategy* covering economic, social and environmental concerns. To implement this strategy, a high level inter-ministerial committee (the Environmental Network) and a National Sustainable Development Partnership (Comhar) have been established. Comhar, which brings together a range of social partners, should have the potential to raise awareness, monitor progress and mobilise public support. Strategic environmental assessment efforts have been undertaken to systematically assess potential impacts of sectoral policies on the environment and sustainable development. Implementation of the new National Development Plan (2000-06) will show how integration efforts are actually to be pursued.

Ireland has recognised the need to reform and strengthen its *spatial planning framework* at the national and regional level. The new Planning and Development Bill, when enacted and implemented, should fill gaps at a subnational level. Strategic planning guidelines for the Dublin Area have shown the way. Systematic analysis of current and future pressures on Ireland's coastal zones, and of policy options to manage their future development and protection, needs to be carried out.

Local Agenda 21s have been initiated. The Environmental Partnership Fund, supporting participatory local co-operation projects, will help broaden the local movement for sustainable development and encourage the activities of NGOs. Overall, administrative initiatives would benefit from increased *participation and partnership* of local community groups and environmental NGOs in the preparation, implementation and monitoring of Local Agenda 21 initiatives.

Improving the cost-effectiveness of environmental policies and strengthening environmental infrastructure

Ireland has a *modern and coherent body of environmental law*. EU environmental law is fully transposed in national law. Most environmental legislation is less than ten years old; the new Planning and Development Bill consolidates physical planning legislation since 1963 and substantially updates spatial planning at the regional and local levels. The *Environmental Protection Agency (EPA)* plays an effective role in implementing environmental policy and monitoring performance, particularly through *Integrated Pollution Control (IPC)* for large industrial plants. The EPA should extend the positive experiences of the *IPC licensing* scheme to a number of activities not yet covered. Co-operation between the *EPA and local authorities* in licensing and enforcement should be fostered, e.g. through training and capacity building. Local authorities are responsible for management of municipal waste, water supply and waste water. For investment purposes they depend to a very large extent upon financing channelled by DOELG, whether the funds come from European sources or national taxpayers. Up until now, Ireland has made only limited use of *economic instruments* to address pollution issues. Eliminating *water charges* for households was a step in the wrong direction. However, Ireland is progressively implementing a comprehensive charging system in respect of non-residential uses. In a period of substantial investment in housing construction, water meters should be installed on new dwellings. Proposals for an increase in energy taxation, balanced by reductions in social charges, have been studied but not yet applied. Targeted compensation payments should be considered for social reasons. The use of *economic instru-*

ments should further help inform polluters and resource users of the true costs of their activities and improve the cost-effectiveness of policies.

In the 1990s, Ireland launched programmes to build waste water collection and treatment facilities with a large share of EU support. Some time will be required to complete these programmes. As important investments in water supply, waste water treatment, waste treatment and air pollution control are still needed, Ireland should step up its national environmental investment effort. Environmental *operating expenditure* will grow. In the 1990s, *environmental expenditure* (pollution abatement and control expenditure, together with that on water supply and nature protection) increased but did not exceed 1% of GDP. Pollution abatement and control expenditure represents 0.6% of GDP, less than in most other OECD countries. Since *EU support* will progressively be phased out as a consequence of its economic performance, Ireland must prepare for a much more significant public and private financial effort with regard to environmental investment and management. Even if the Irish budget situation has improved, environmental expenditure will increasingly need to be covered by *charges* levied on polluters and resource users. Recent public-private partnerships in water services (e.g. build-operate-transfer projects) are steps in this direction. The introduction of *revenue neutral eco-taxation* should be a subject in the new partnership agreement among the social partners.

In the 1990s, Ireland renovated its *environmental monitoring and reporting capacity* (e.g. State of the Environment reports, environmental indicators) and set up effective arrangements to translate into practice *public access to environmental information* (e.g. access to licenses, EIA processes and courts). The national environmental information centre *(ENFO)* provides valuable free access to a wide range of environment related information and is particularly active in environmental education. This valuable initiative should be brought to the attention of other countries.

6

SECTORAL INTEGRATION: TRANSPORT

1. Transport Activities and the Environment

Current situation and trends

Ireland's *peripheral island location* contributes to the heavy reliance of its open economy on transport for importing and exporting goods. In addition, *recent demographic and economic trends* (population growth, growing number of households and rising income levels) are manifested in urban sprawl and increasing demand for personal mobility. In the Dublin metropolitan area, where nearly 40% of the population lives, meeting freight and passenger demand presents transport, environmental and economic challenges.

Transportation networks and fleets

The *road network* totals 96 000 kilometres, including 103 kilometres of national motorways and 2 749 kilometres of primary roads. Reflecting the historical pattern of rural development, the density of Ireland's road network is higher than the OECD Europe average (Figure 6.1). However, the density of the *motorway system* is only about 10% of the average for OECD Europe. The overall quality of Ireland's roads is lower than in most OECD countries.

The density of the *railway system* (2.8 kilometres/100 km^2) is 30% lower than the OECD Europe average. Railway lines total 2 000 kilometres, including 520 kilometres of double track and about 40 kilometres of suburban electrified line.

Private car ownership (32 per 100 people; 35 in the Dublin region) has increased by 50% since 1990 and is approaching the OECD Europe average (Figure 6.1). In 1998, the national fleet consisted of nearly 1.5 million vehicles (including 1.2 million passenger cars and 174 000 goods vehicles). The passenger car fleet is relatively new; the average age is seven years, and less than 2% is

Figure 6.1 Trends in the transport sector

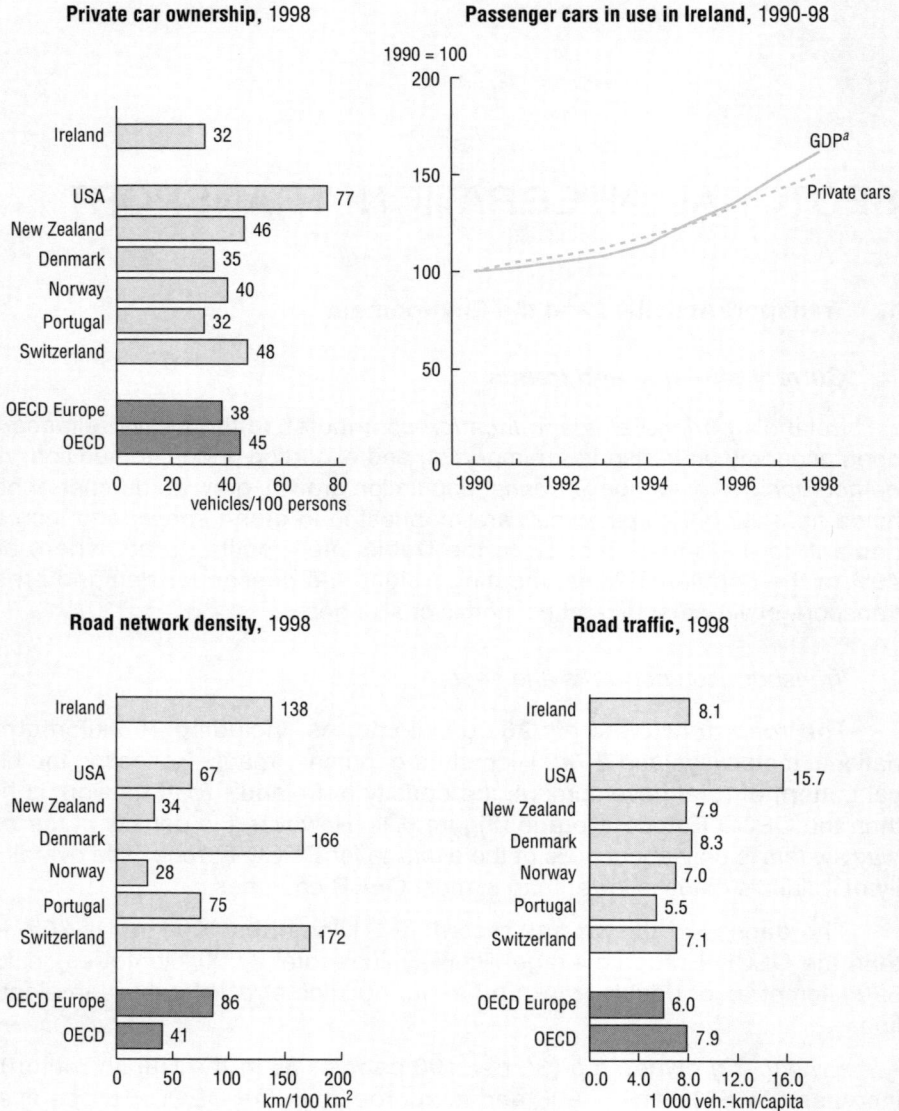

Private car ownership, 1998

Ireland 32
USA 77
New Zealand 46
Denmark 35
Norway 40
Portugal 32
Switzerland 48

OECD Europe 38
OECD 45

0   20   40   60   80
vehicles/100 persons

Passenger cars in use in Ireland, 1990-98

1990 = 100

GDP^a
Private cars

200

150

100

50

0

1990   1992   1994   1996   1998

Road network density, 1998

Ireland 138
USA 67
New Zealand 34
Denmark 166
Norway 28
Portugal 75
Switzerland 172

OECD Europe 86
OECD 41

0   50   100   150   200
km/100 km^2

Road traffic, 1998

Ireland 8.1
USA 15.7
New Zealand 7.9
Denmark 8.3
Norway 7.0
Portugal 5.5
Switzerland 7.1

OECD Europe 6.0
OECD 7.9

0.0   4.0   8.0   12.0   16.0
1 000 veh.-km/capita

a)   GDP at 1991 prices and purchasing power parities.
Source: IRF; AAMA; OECD.

over 16 years old. The number of *goods vehicles* registered in Ireland has increased by over 10% since 1990; over 95% of goods vehicles use diesel fuel.

Dublin's public transport system consists of some 950 buses and four public transit rail lines (Dublin Area Rapid Transit, or DART). The bus network is partially integrated with the DART and has a number of links to DART stations. In most *other municipalities*, public transport is limited to buses.

Freight transport

About 64% of Ireland's *international shipment of freight*, by value, passes through seaports; the remainder passes through airports (20%) or crosses the land frontier (16%). Two *seaports* (Dublin and Dun Laoghaire) account for 63% of total foreign trade volume. Other important ports include Cork, Waterford and Rosslare. The volume of goods handled at Irish seaports has more than doubled since 1990. At the port of Dublin, freight traffic has increased in volume by 136% since 1991, reaching 18.2 million tonnes in 1999.

Air shipment is important to foreign trade in high-value goods. When the value of the freight is considered, *nearly 20% of foreign trade by value passes through airports*, mostly consisting of high value-added small components (e.g. electronic parts or computer chips). Air freight is growing rapidly, with throughput at the three State airports (Dublin, Shannon, Cork) increasing by over 6% per year since 1989.

In 1997, modal share (in tonne-kilometres) for *internal freight shipping* was 91% by road and 9% by rail. Since 1990, the volume of freight shipped by rail has fallen by 19% with road transport picking up the slack.

Passenger transport

Air travel accounts for 75% of total *passenger transport to and from Ireland* and sea travel for 25%. Overall passenger demand has nearly tripled since 1990, and this rapid increase is expected to continue with economic expansion. Passenger traffic at *Dublin airport* (9 million in 1996) has increased by 116% since 1991 and represents over 75% of the national total. Over 4 million international passengers per year travel to or from Ireland by sea; 60% debark in the Dublin region (41% at Dun Laoghaire port and 19% at Dublin port).

Road travel is the dominant mode of *domestic passenger transport*; passenger vehicles account for 82% of passenger-kilometres travelled and buses for 14%. Overall *road traffic per capita* is 35% higher than the OECD Europe average (Figure 6.1). Rail accounts for about 3% of passenger-kilometres, with railways, which provide passenger service to Dublin, Cork, Limerick and Galway, carrying an estimated 30 million passengers per year.

The percentage of passenger journeys via urban *public transport* has been decreasing since the mid 1980s, though the absolute number has remained relatively constant. In the *Dublin region*, public transport's share has fallen by 6% since 1988; however, public transport still accommodates nearly 25% of total passenger trips (over 88 000 daily boardings and approximately 170 million passenger-kilometres per year).

Pressures on the environment

Air emissions

The *transport sector* is a major source of *air emissions*. Combined emissions from Irish transport (all modes) represent 82% of CO, 49% of NO_x and 5% of SO_2 emissions (Table 6.1). Energy use by the transport sector (34% of TFC) is roughly equal to the OECD Europe average but is growing rapidly. *Road transport* contributes 80% of CO, 41% of NO_x and 18% of CO_2 emissions. With the projected rapid growth of the road vehicle fleet, road transport's share of national air emissions is expected to continue to grow.

Lead emissions, which are almost entirely from road transport, have been dramatically reduced since 1990 and will essentially cease in 2000 with the phase-out of leaded fuel (Chapter 3). The average ambient lead concentration in Dublin is 0.13 $\mu g/m^3$, well below the 2.0 $\mu g/m^3$ standard.

Noise

Noise nuisance from road traffic is an increasing concern in urban areas. Data on the number of persons exposed to unacceptable levels are not available.

Table 6.1 **Transport emissions to air,** 1990-98

	% of national emissions originating from transport		
	1990	1994	1998
CO	75.7	79.5	81.9
NO_x	39.6	41.2	49.2
SO_2	3.7	4.8	5.4

Source: DOELG; OECD.

Noise from air traffic is not seen as a major problem, since abatement measures have been taken at all major airports.

Use of land and resources

Land use by transport infrastructure, which has expanded rapidly in recent years, contributes to the fragmentation and destruction of ecosystems and natural habitats.

Disposal of waste from the transport sector entails managing scrapped vehicles, used tyres, batteries and oil products. Widespread importation of used tyres and vehicles contributes heavily to transport-related waste disposal problems.

Accidents and health risks

The *severity and frequency of traffic accidents* have decreased since 1996. The annual rate of fatal transport-related accidents (121 deaths per million inhabitants) is about equal to the OECD Europe average, but road fatalities per million private cars (441) is 1.5 times the OECD Europe average. Alcohol is involved in 33% of fatal accidents.

Risks associated with transport of hazardous waste and oil products raise concern because of the potential scale and intensity of an accident. Ireland has taken preparatory measures to respond to oil spills in offshore areas (Chapter 7). As a major source of air emissions, the transport sector contributes to respiratory health problems. Few exposure data are available.

2. Responses

The *Department of the Environment and Local Government (DOELG)* is responsible for defining and implementing road transport policy. The *Department of Marine and National Resources* is responsible for port management, and the *Department of Public Enterprise* for public transport, railways and aviation. Fiscal policy relating to roads and fuels is the responsibility of the *Department of Finance*.

The *National Roads Authority (NRA)*, a statutory authority of DOELG created in 1994, is responsible for maintenance and expansion of national primary and secondary roads (totalling 5 400 kilometres). The NRA makes funds available to carry out this work through local authorities. In addition, *local authorities* are directly responsible for maintaining over 90 000 kilometres of local roads (assisted by the local government fund and local taxes).

Transport policy objectives relating to the environment

The *Roads Act of 1993* established the NRA and provided a comprehensive procedure for environmental impact assessment of all road projects likely to have significant environmental effects. An environmental impact statement must be submitted at the time of project application; the public has the right to participate in the review process at several stages.

The *Operational Programme for Transport* (OPT) (1994-99) included provisions for substantial EU-supported investment in transport infrastructure (EUR 3 229 million). The programme's stated objectives were to improve internal transport infrastructure, and to increase the operational efficiency of transport systems by remedying bottlenecks and capacity deficiencies. It sought to reduce overall environmental impacts through investments in energy efficiency and the operational speed of rail transport (both passenger and freight traffic) and to encourage further public transport development.

The *National Roads Authority Statement of Strategy* (1999-2002) sets the objective of taking an integrated approach to transport planning, using land use planning as a tool to manage transport demand. While prioritising construction and amelioration of needed infrastructure, the strategy also aims to optimise the efficiency of the existing road network using traffic management approaches. In addition, the strategy calls for more accurate estimation of the environmental externalities of transport and major road schemes.

The *Dublin Transportation Initiative (DTI)* (1992-99) sought to develop an integrated approach to surface transport (road, rail, bus, cycling, walking) in the Dublin region, giving high priority to development of public transport options. A significant updating of the DTI Strategy was launched in 2000. The DTI's overall approach has been to improve integration of transport policies with those on land use, economic development, urban renewal, employment and the environment.

The Government's *Road to Safety Strategy (1998-2002)* has the objective of reducing Irish road fatalities in 2002 by at least 20% relative to their 1998 level. A similar reduction is sought in the number of serious injuries resulting from road accidents. The strategy sets additional specific targets for 2002, including reduction of speeding (by 50%) and increased use of front and rear seat belts (by at least 85%).

Measures for transport infrastructure investment

Public investment in *road construction* has grown more rapidly than general public investment since 1990, boosted by EU funding. Total investment in transport under the 1989-93 Operational Programme on Peripherality (OPP), predecessor of the OPT, was approximately IEP 990 million. Between 1994 and 1999,

IEP 1 655 million was dedicated to road development (Table 6.2). Most of this amount was for improvements to the national motorway network.

Since 1994, Ireland has begun giving some priority to investment in its *railway system*, with IEP 275 million invested in the framework of the OPT (Table 6.2).

Investment in *Dublin's public transport system* is receiving increasing priority (Table 6.2). Between 1989 and 1993, IEP 48 million (7% of total transport investment) was allocated to public transport; between 1994 and 1999, this increased to IEP 356 million (14% of total transport investment). Investment has mainly been aimed at expanding light rail and suburban rail systems and creating quality bus corridors (QBCs) and bicycle lanes.

Environmental impact statements (EIS) are carried out for all transport projects that could have significant environmental impacts. The local authority prepares a detailed EIS for any such project, which is submitted to DOELG with an application for project approval. *Public notice* must be given; the general public and certain specified organisations have the opportunity to make written submissions to the Minister. Public hearings on likely environmental impacts are held for certain projects and are mandatory for all motorway projects. Between 1988 and 1996, about 100 EIS were submitted for transport projects.

Table 6.2 **Transport investment,**[a] 1994-99

	Investment (IEP million[b])	(%)
Roads	1 655	*63*
Airports	225	*9*
Seaports	94	*4*
Rail	275	*10*
Public transport	356	*14*
Total	2 605	*100*

a) Total investment from Regional Fund, Cohesion Fund and national resources.
b) 1994 IEP.
Source: OPT, 1994-99.

Measures relating to vehicles and fuels

Concerning vehicle *emission standards*, Ireland has ensured the full and timely implementation of relevant EU directives. *Noise limits* are imposed on road, railway, waterborne and airborne traffic, and *noise standards* are applied for aircraft.

Limited *emissions testing* of both light- and heavy-goods vehicles has been carried out since 1988. The pollutants tested for have included CO and smoke. A more comprehensive yearly inspection of passenger cars (including second-hand imports) for exhaust emissions will become mandatory in 2000 under the *National Car Test (NCT) system*, created in conformity with EU Directive 96/96/EC. The NCT, to be phased in between 2000 and 2002, will be applied first to the oldest vehicles. Testing, performed every two years, will cost owners IEP 35.

A vehicle scrapping programme, implemented between 1995 and 1997, was intended to reduce the number of old passenger cars in the Irish fleet. Under this scheme, anyone who scrapped a car over ten years old and purchased a new one within one month benefited from an IEP 1 000 reduction of the Vehicle Registration Tax (VRT), representing about 5% of the full price of the vehicle. During this programme, 61 000 vehicles were scrapped, some 6% of the fleet.

Since 1997, efforts have been made to equip Dublin with *less-polluting and more energy-efficient buses*. In 1999, 150 new diesel-fuelled buses were purchased; one CNG bus and one LPG bus were in use. Coras Iompair Eireann (CIE), the government monopoly that provides bus and rail service throughout Ireland, estimates that such measures resulted in a 10% reduction of its operations' specific energy consumption between 1993 and 2000.

Ireland's *fuel quality standards* for petrol and diesel meet EU norms (Chapter 3). Unleaded fuel had a 7% market share in 1989, increasing to 92% in 1999. Complete phase-out of leaded petrol was accomplished in 1999. The maximum allowable sulphur content of diesel fuel was reduced to 500 ppm in 1996, and to 350 ppm in 2000; a further reduction to 50 ppm is planned for January 2005.

Ireland's *vehicle fuel prices* are lower than those in neighbouring OECD Europe countries (Table 6.3). Adjusted for purchasing power parities, the price of unleaded premium in 1998 was about 10% less than the average for France, Germany, the Netherlands and the United Kingdom, and about 11% below the overall OECD Europe average. At 1998 prices and exchange rates, the *price of diesel fuel* in Ireland was 30% lower than in the UK. While the excise duty on leaded and super unleaded was increased by 4 pence per litre in 1998, the share of taxes in the pump price of motor vehicle fuels remains relatively low compared to other OECD Europe countries.

Figure 6.2   **Road fuel prices and taxes**

Trends in Ireland,[a] 1990-98

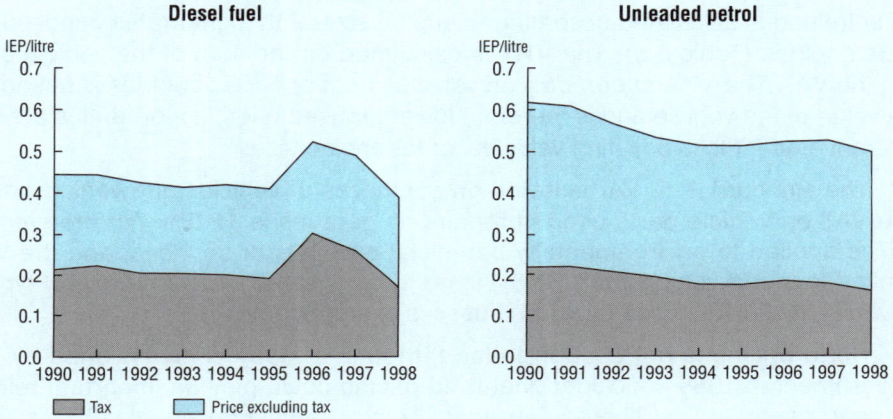

Diesel fuel

Unleaded petrol

☐ Tax   ☐ Price excluding tax

a)   At constant 1991 prices.
Source :   IEA-OECD.

Table 6.3   **Transport fuel prices,** 1998
(USD/litre)

	Diesel[a]		Unleaded premium[b]	
	Price	% tax	Price	% tax
Ireland	0.652	56.7	0.847	68.0
France	0.593	69.5	0.926	81.2
Germany	0.559	63.1	0.792	75.2
Greece	0.433	59.1	0.888	66.7
Netherlands	0.617	61.1	1.021	74.9
Portugal	0.532	57.9	1.296	72.9
United Kingdom	0.922	78.6	0.988	81.5
Irish price/OECD Europe	106%	. .	89%	. .

a)   At current prices and exchange rates.
b)   RON 95 at current prices and PPPs.
Source: IEA-OECD.

Economic instruments

Instruments relating to car ownership

The *vehicle registration tax (VRT)* imposed for first-time registration of a vehicle in Ireland is calculated according to engine size, with higher rates imposed on large engines (Table 5.5). The VRT is calculated on the sum of the vehicle cost and the VAT. The 10% *import duty* on vehicles from non-EU countries is based on the value of the vehicle and is therefore lower for used ones; import duties are not differentiated for less polluting vehicles, or for engine size.

The standard *21% VAT* is levied on purchases of vehicles and vehicle parts. The VAT on vehicle parts used in repairs by garages is 12.5%. *No preferential VAT* is applied to environmentally beneficial products or services, and the VAT applied to motor vehicle fuels (21%) is not differentiated according to fuel types. However, diesel fuel used by public buses is exempt from VAT.

Road pricing is not used in Ireland, though a study commissioned by the Government in 1999 concluded that road pricing could play an important role in future transport policy. There is an *annual motor vehicle tax* on all vehicles, and the tax on cars is differentiated in favour of smaller engines (Table 5.5). Those with small engines (1 001-1 500 cc) are taxed at IEP 13.3 per 100 cc; more powerful ones (2 501-3 000 cc) at IEP 23.3 per 100 cc. Owners of electric cars and those with engine capacity below 1 000 cc pay the same flat tax of IEP 98. The annual tax on goods vehicles, based on unladen weight, ranges between IEP 160 (less than 3 tonnes) and IEP 2 494 (over 20 tonnes).

Instruments relating to car use

Differentiated *excise taxes* on leaded and unleaded petrol were effective in facilitating phase-out of leaded fuel. Lower excise taxes are applied to diesel and LPG (Table 5.5). In the late 1990s, taxation represented 68% of the pump price of petrol and 57% of that of diesel (Table 6.3 and Figure 6.2). Some of these tax revenues (IEP 980.7 million in 1997) go to the *Local Government Fund*, where they are allocated to activities such as road maintenance and construction.

Income tax provisions do not encourage passenger car commuting: use of a company car is treated as a taxable benefit, and commuting expenses are not deductible for income tax purposes. As of 1999, public transport passes provided by employers are not considered, for fiscal purposes, as in-kind benefits.

In 1998, a comprehensive system of *parking charges and restrictions* was implemented for central Dublin and some other congested areas. There are increasing restrictions on free on-street parking in the city, and enforcement is vigorous (fines of IEP 15-65 per offense, routine wheel clamping). All newly constructed parking facilities must be multi-storey. Electronic bulletin boards around the city indicate the number of parking spaces available in over 30 parking garages. To discourage all-day parking, parking rates in garages are graduated. Parking spaces made available to employees free of charge are not currently treated as a taxable benefit.

Other instruments

Product charges are not applied to tyres, oils or lubricants to help finance their disposal. One private company in Dublin, which pays garages IEP 1 for each battery collected, carries out reclamation of car batteries. Acids from the batteries are recycled; solid materials are crushed and exported. A private company also recycles used oils, but garages pay for this service. Garages may burn used oils for heating only with a special permit (annual cost approximately IEP 5 000).

Regulatory and other measures for traffic management

Since 1997, Dublin has implemented a system of *environmental traffic cells* as a traffic management measure. Through traffic is limited in cells designated for non-public vehicles.

Three dedicated bus lanes or "quality bus corridors" (QBCs) operate in Dublin (15 kilometres). The objective of the QBC initiative, begun in 1998, is to encourage bus use by ensuring significant time savings to passengers. Where QBCs are operational, passengers report time savings of about 30%. A strong effort to create *bicycle lanes* had resulted in a network of 25 kilometres in 1999. They are still being expanded.

Computerised traffic management (the SCATS system) is used to optimise the Dublin traffic situation, giving priority to pedestrian and bicycle traffic to the greatest extent possible. It has led to a 4% increase in the number of vehicles handled and helped reduce congestion. Electronic traffic control is also used in some smaller cities, including Cork.

Strategic Planning Guidelines and Residential Density Guidelines were issued for the Greater Dublin Area in 1999. These guidelines seek to integrate traffic management efforts into planning. A country-wide cap on *maximum allowable retail space* (3 000 square metres) was imposed in 1999, in an attempt to limit siting of large shopping centres on the periphery of urban areas. This measure is designed in part to reduce demand for personal mobility.

Since the early 1990s, the Government has actively imposed *traffic safety regulations* that include lower speed limits and seat belt requirements. Between 1990 and 1998, the number of persons killed annually in road accidents fell by 5%, despite a considerable increase in the number of vehicles used and in average distances travelled.

3.   Progress Towards Sustainability of the Transport Sector

Ireland is seeking to upgrade and expand its *transport infrastructure and services,* which are considered important in regard to economic development, European integration and the quality of life of its citizens. During the recent period of rapid economic growth, *road transport's domination of the modal split* has been accompanied by decreases in the shares of rail and public transport. Improving transport infrastructure usually stimulates demand, and recent investments in road construction have undoubtedly encouraged use of road transport to some extent. However, improvements in national road infrastructure have been justified. Ireland is actively seeking to balance this growth with improvements in urban transport systems and railways.

Infrastructure

As a result of rapid economic growth, there is an urgent *need to expand transport infrastructure*, particularly motorways, high-quality dual carriageways, public transport, and their links with major ports and airports. This need is being addressed through use of EU and national public funding. Since 1995, the majority of public investment in transport has been oriented towards *construction of national motorways and roads*. Maintaining the extensive local road network remains a major challenge for local authorities. To date, public-private partnerships have been under-utilised as a means of providing investment in transport infrastructure, and the User-Pays Principle has only been very weakly implemented.

Investment in the national *railways* has been one of the priorities under the Operational Programme for Transport (OPT). However, railway development potential is limited to a few lines due to certain characteristics of Irish industry (dispersed industrial sites, prevalence of just-in-time management approaches) and the country's population distribution (one principal urban centre). Upgrading the Belfast-Dublin line and other lines within the Republic is being given priority, mainly as a way to reduce freight shipping by road. Investment in *public transport* has increased dramatically in Dublin and Cork since 1994. Nevertheless, implementation difficulties, primarily relating to land use conflicts, have delayed specific projects considerably.

EIA procedures are well-established in Ireland and are routinely applied to major transport projects. An EIS precedes motorway construction, and project alternatives appear to be given adequate consideration. Public participation also appears active, but transport authorities have urged that project review processes be simplified to facilitate timely implementation.

Looking ahead, continued financial requirements for investment and the increasing need for operation and maintenance funds, coupled with reduced EU funding, will call for wider development of public-private partnerships and more appropriate pricing of services provided to users.

Vehicles, fuels and traffic

Ireland's transport sector is a major source of air emissions, accounting for 60% of VOCs, 82% of CO, 49% of NO_x and 5% of SO_2 emissions (Table 6.1). Energy use by the transport sector (34% of TFC) is roughly equal to the OECD Europe average but is increasing rapidly. Road transport contributes 80% of CO, 41% of NO_x and 18% of CO_2 emissions; with continued rapid expansion of the road vehicle fleet, its share of national air emissions can also be expected to grow.

Ireland has implemented *EU vehicle and fuel standards* in time and effectively. Progressive phase-out of leaded fuel was completed in 1999. A vehicle-scrapping programme aimed at reducing the number of old vehicles was effective, ridding the fleet of 61 000 vehicles (some 6% of the total fleet). However, comprehensive emissions testing for in-use vehicles has been delayed, with implementation taking place from 2000.

Since 1997, *wide-ranging traffic management measures* in the Dublin region (environmental traffic cells, parking management, dedicated bus corridors) have helped significantly to reduce congestion. A system of *parking charges and restrictions* has also contributed to controlling urban congestion. This is particularly true in Dublin, where they have been well-organised and effectively enforced. Future effectiveness will depend on continued vigorous enforcement.

Land use planning and *integration of planning and traffic management* objectives have been historically weak in Ireland. This has been partially responsible for urban sprawl and the increased demand for personal mobility. In the Dublin area, the 1999 Strategic Planning Guidelines may help confront this problem. At the national level, the need to co-ordinate responses to rapidly increasing international freight movements and passenger traffic has not yet been adequately addressed. Over-concentration of traffic in the Dublin area is a result.

Looking ahead, while decisions taken in the latter part of the 1990s will have benefits, Ireland's likely sustained economic growth will continue to generate freight traffic increases, urban sprawl (associated with rising income levels and inadequate land use planning) and growing personal mobility demand. This presents serious challenges in regard to environmental protection and sustainable development.

Economic signals

Whereas the Operational Programme for Transport has prioritised construction of infrastructure to meet demand, a range of *economic instruments* are used to manage demand for road transport and to internalise some of its negative externalities. Motor vehicle fuel taxes account for 57-68% of the pump price of vehicle fuels; fuel prices are lower than in neighbouring countries.

In 1997, 13.5% of total government revenue was raised through *road user taxation*, equivalent to nearly 2% of GDP. Together the vehicle registration tax, value added tax and vehicle sales tax constitute high taxation of vehicle ownership (in the range of 75-93% of the vehicle's value, depending on engine size). Overall, taxes are disproportionately targeted at *vehicle ownership* rather than *vehicle use*: once the hurdle of ownership is overcome, there is no strong brake on use. A review of the overall taxation scheme might therefore be useful.

Some *economic measures* are used to encourage the purchase of *smaller and cleaner vehicles* (vehicle sales, fuel and registration taxes). Income tax rules do not favour passenger car commuting, and public transport passes provided by employers are not treated as an in-kind benefit. The rate of *subsidisation of public transport* in Ireland (3-10%) is lower than in many other OECD countries, and public opinion polls indicate that tariffs are presently considered high. Adjustment of public transport tariffs through employers' contributions or further subsidisation should be further reviewed, as a means to improve competitiveness with other forms of transport. Incentives to encourage purchase of vehicles that use alternative fuels for public transport might also be considered. Product charges and road pricing are not yet used to internalise economic externalities associated with vehicle operation. There are no incentives to recycle or reclaim *transport-related wastes* (batteries, used oil and tyres), and negative incentives often exist.

Part III

CO-OPERATION WITH
THE INTERNATIONAL COMMUNITY

7

INTERNATIONAL CO-OPERATION

During the last 15 years, Ireland has developed international environmental co-operation activities as a *full partner* of the other EU Member States. Its environmental policies correspond to those of its main partners. This is consistent with the economic importance of exports of goods and services (82% of GDP), EU financial support and increasing foreign direct investment. In a period of rapid growth, much progress on environmental protection has been driven by EU legislation and funding, as well as by implementation of *international agreements*. Ireland also wishes to maintain its image as a *"green" country*, which is of particular importance in view of the economic significance of its agricultural exports and international tourism.

As part of meeting the goal of sustainable development, the Irish Government's current strategy is to *"contribute as effectively as possible to international efforts* to protect the environment and to deal with global/regional environmental problems, particularly acidification, climate change and ozone layer depletion and implement relevant conclusions of the processes".

1. Integration in the European Union and Bilateral Co-operation

Transposition of EU directives

Ireland has *transposed most EU environmental directives* (98%) and compares very favourably with other Member States in this regard. A few directives nevertheless cause difficulties.

The *drinking water* of a small percentage of the population is still microbiologically contaminated. Over 50 000 households served by private group water schemes in rural areas will benefit from improvements in water supply through the Rural Water Programme (IEP 33 million in 1999). However, the national objective of full compliance with EU drinking water criteria by the end of 1999 is unlikely to have been achieved. A package of measures was announced in March 2000 to

138

tackle the water quality problems confronting the group water sector, including an investment of IEP 430 million to improve rural water infrastructure over the period 2000-06 and a major revamp of grant and subsidy schemes.

Concerning the *habitat directive*, Ireland has provided a first list of protected sites but not yet the whole list. Thus, the European Commission cannot ascertain whether a proposed development would affect a site that should be protected.

Concerning the *urban waste water directive*, very large efforts to build new treatment plants (over IEP 1 billion) have been launched covering 116 municipalities.

The European Court of Justice found in 1999 that Ireland had not properly implemented the provisions of the 1985 *EIA directive* in relation to peat extraction and afforestation. Legal steps are also being taken by the European Commission regarding transposition of directives on waste management and animal experiments.

EU funding

Ireland has received considerable EU funding under various schemes, including *Structural and Cohesion funds and the Common Agricultural Policy* (Table 7.1). Net transfers in 1997 were almost *EUR 2.7 billion (over 4% of GDP)*

Table 7.1 **EU transfers**, 1998[a]

	Agricultural aid (A)	Structural and Cohesion funds (B)	EU expenditure[b] (C)	Contribution to EU budget (D)	Net EU transfers (C-D)	Net EU transfer per capita	Net EU transfer % of GDP	GDP per capita[c]
	EUR billion	EUR billion	EUR billion	EUR billion	EUR billion	EUR	%	EUR
Ireland	1.64 (4.2%)	1.48 (5.2%)	3.44	0.98 (1.2%)	2.46	664	3.2	21 680
Greece	2.56 (6.6%)	3.23 (11.4%)	6.35	1.31 (1.6%)	5.04	479	4.6	13 340
Portugal	0.64 (1.6%)	3.22 (11.3%)	4.26	1.10 (1.3%)	3.16	317	3.2	15 060
Spain	5.30 (13.7%)	6.83 (24.1%)	13.27	5.75 (7%)	7.52	191	1.4	16 300
Total EU	38.81	28.36	80.72	82.25				

a) Figures in brackets are % of EU total.
b) A + B + administrative expenditure + non-EU expenses.
c) At 1998 PPP.
Source: EU.

or EUR 723 per capita, the highest level in Europe. Large infrastructure is financed up to 85% by the Structural and Cohesion funds. EU agricultural support has had a significant impact on farming practices. In some cases, it has encouraged overgrazing and therefore damaged the environment; in others it has helped preserve the landscape through avoiding intensification.

There is substantial *EU funding of environmental infrastructure*. Ireland has participated in INTERREG programmes and in the LIFE programme. In connection with EU directives on drinking water and urban waste water treatment, it has the goal of securing "provision of the water and waste water services necessary for environmental and for economic and regional development purposes". Water supply and sanitation has received the most EU funding (over IEP 1 billion between 1994 and 1999). Support has also been provided for waste management, nature protection and climate change. Between 2000 and 2006, investment in waste, sewerage and waste water treatment services (IEP 3 billion) will need some level of EU support.

Co-operation with Northern Ireland

Ireland is carrying out a series of environmental protection projects with Northern Ireland that affect the *whole island* or the *boundary regions*. These include:

- management of hospital waste for the entire island by a single contractor, appointed by a joint waste management board;

- submission of waste management plans to local authorities across the border;

- notification by the EPA of activities which could have an impact on trans-frontier groundwater;

- studies on the management of the Erne system and the estuary of Lough Foyle;

- liaison between Departments of the Environment on EIAs involving trans-boundary effects;

- emergency planning for emergencies in boundary regions;

- development of a biodiversity action plan in boundary regions.

A bilateral agreement on EIA is being negotiated. Ireland is ready to ratify the 1991 Espoo Convention; it will consider ratifying the 1992 Helsinki Convention on transboundary accidents and the 1992 Helsinki Convention on transboundary watercourses, which are aimed at *strengthening transboundary co-operation*.

Co-operation with the United Kingdom

In addition to co-operation with Northern Ireland, Ireland's *co-operation with the United Kingdom* is particularly strong on *radioactivity and marine issues.* Meetings between Irish and UK authorities on radioactivity-related matters are held twice a year. In addition, there are meetings between Irish authorities and those in Northern Ireland on monitoring the radioactivity of the sea. Close co-operation at scientific and operational levels exists between Irish scientists and officials and their counterparts in the UK (particularly Wales, the Isle of Man, Scotland). In the framework of INTERREG Programmes, joint research activities are carried out by Ireland and Wales concerning protection of the marine environment and marine emergency planning.

2. Protection of the Marine Environment

Coastal activities

Ireland has *7 100 kilometres of coastline.* More than *half its population* lives in coastal areas. Some areas of coastline are threatened by erosion: 1 500 kilometres is at risk, and 490 kilometres requires immediate action.

Sea fisheries (fish, mussels, oysters, sea urchins) give employment to 16 000 people and generate IEP 118 million in loadings from 1 400 vessels. The total allowable catch has fallen since 1991 and certain fish stocks are declining. *Aquaculture* (salmon, rainbow trout) is rapidly growing; production increased from IEP 40 million to IEP 103 million between 1993 and 1999. Over 2 500 people work in aquaculture, which accounts for 25% of Irish fish production. It is very vulnerable to pollution and is itself a source of pollution. Many shellfish areas have been affected by faecal pollution. *Tourism* activities are expanding rapidly (over 8% per year), especially in coastal areas. In 1998, tourism employed 126 700 people and accounted for 5% of exports. Foreign tourist inflow increased from 1.9 million in 1984 to 5.5 million in 1998.

Marine and coastal biodiversity is threatened by new housing construction and other polluting activities in coastal areas, and by sea pollution from land-based sources. The Irish Government issued a discussion document in 1997 outlining a *policy for integrated coastal management.* Public consultation took place during 1998, and a National Strategy for National Coastal Zone Management was expected to be released in 2000 by the three Irish departments concerned (Marine, Environment, Heritage). The objective is to preserve the most valuable remaining areas in terms of biodiversity. The Strategy, based on a participatory approach, will involve the County Councils.

Land-based marine pollution

Irish *beaches* have been designated with Blue Flags (19 in 1988, 77 in 1999) in recognition of their overall quality. The vast majority of monitored beaches conform to the EU *bathing water* directive; cases of non-compliance fell from 5.6% in 1992 to 1.6% in 1998.

Localised marine pollution occurs along the sea coast *near estuaries of large cities and waste water outfalls*. Non-compliance is mostly related to bacterial pollution (faecal coliforms) resulting from poor treatment of urban waste water; some shellfish areas are polluted for the same reason. Improvements are expected when waste water treatment plants planned or under construction become operational, i.e. when the Irish Environmental Policy's target of 80% secondary treatment is met. So far, about 22% of collected waters receive secondary treatment. Most sewage is still discharged (untreated or after primary treatment only) to estuarine or coastal waters. While the Irish Environmental Policy has included the goal of full compliance with the EU bathing water directive by the end of the decade, it is clear that this will only be achieved when the new treatment plants are in operation.

Ireland was a party to the Oslo and Paris Conventions. It is now a party to the 1992 OSPAR Convention. Ireland and the United Kingdom jointly prepared a Quality Status Report for the *Celtic Seas Region*, submitted to OSPAR in August 1999. Ireland has also been participating with UK authorities in preparing a Directory of the Coastal Margin of the Celtic Seas. This Directory, to be published in mid 2000, will provide a comprehensive description of habitats and species.

In 1987, Ireland banned the use of *tributyltin* (TBT) as an anti-fouling agent on vessels less than 25 metres long and on structures in water. This measure was very useful in aquaculture areas, but had little effect in harbours for large ships.

Dumping at sea

Ireland protects the marine environment in the 200-mile *fishery zone* (465 000 km^2) and on its *continental shelf* (99 000 km^2). As a party to the Oslo and London Dumping Conventions, it prohibited dumping of *industrial waste* in 1993. Incineration of substances at sea is forbidden, as is disposal at sea of toxic, harmful and noxious substances or of radioactive waste. In 1996, the Government abolished dumping of *ammunition* in Irish waters and waved its right under the sovereign immunity provision of the OSPAR Convention.

In 1997, 12 permits were issued for dumping of *dredged material* (625 000 tonnes), *sewage sludge* (23 000 tonnes) and *fish waste* (420 tonnes). The overall amount of waste authorised for dumping is decreasing; there were only nine permits in 1999. Disposal of sewage sludge at sea was prohibited in 1999. The only waste which may still be dumped is dredged material from capital and maintenance works at harbours.

Ireland expressed strong concern about *dumping of radioactive waste* in the Atlantic between 1950 and 1990, in part under OECD-NEA supervision. It actively supported adoption of the moratorium (subsequently ban) on radioactive waste dumping at sea.

Transfrontier marine pollution

The discharge to the Irish Sea of *radioactive effluents* from the Sellafield, UK, reprocessing plant caused limited radioactive pollution of the sea, as well as considerable anxiety in Ireland. As the radioactive releases were strongly reduced, radioactive concentration of Cs 137 dropped from 40 Bq/kg in 1982 to less than 0.8 Bq/kg in 1992; however, Tc 99 concentration has increased. Scientists of both countries consider that no significant health risk is posed by consuming fish from the Irish Sea. The Irish Government advocates closing this installation.

During the 1990s, on both the UK and Irish coasts, some of the Second World War *ammunition* dumped by the UK between 1945 and 1963 in its Beaufort Dyke was still present. Surveys were carried out in both countries and at sea, to investigate associated risks and to fully inventory Irish Sea chemical ammunition dump sites.

Maritime traffic

Ireland is trying to strengthen surveillance of the maritime traffic of *hazardous or radioactive material cargoes* near its coasts. Regulations were adopted in 1999 to transpose the EU Hazmat directive, which requires all vessels carrying dangerous or polluting goods bound for or leaving a EU port to notify national authorities. Ireland is discussing, on a bilateral basis, arrangements for voyages of vessels carrying hazardous or radioactive cargoes (notably with countries that send radioactive waste for reprocessing to Sellafield). It hopes to be kept informed about all ships carrying radioactive waste in the Irish Sea; such ships are seen as presenting a risk. Ireland also hopes that the existing Code of Safe Carriage of Irradiated Nuclear Fuel will become mandatory, and that countries will agree to implement a very strict new code for shipment of nuclear material.

Facilities have been installed in all ports to receive *ships' waste*. Consequently, Ireland has been able to accede to MARPOL.

Oil spills and liability for maritime accidents

In recent years, Ireland has experienced about 15 minor *oil spills* per year. A few of these damaged beaches. Major spills have involved the Betelgeuse in

Bantry Bay (10 000 tonnes in 1979), the Kowloon Bridge off Cork (1 700 tonnes in 1986) and the Sea Empress at Milford Haven (UK) (72 000 tonnes in 1996).

Between 1994 and 1997, 78 accidents occurred involving 32 cargo vessels, 13 tankers, eight bulk carriers and eight ferries. The *Irish Marine Emergency Service* (IMES), established in 1991, is responsible for marine emergency preparedness and response. It operates equipment stored at national bases that can cope with a 5 000 tonne spill. If the spill is larger, additional equipment can be provided by private contractors in the UK; assistance can also be obtained in the framework of the Bonn Agreement or of the EU.

Ireland participates in many IMO activities. It is an observer for the Bonn Agreement on prevention of oil pollution in the North Sea, as well as a member of the EU Advisory Committee on Pollution by Hydrocarbons and other harmful substances discharged at sea (ACPH). In 1999, *Ireland ratified* the 1990 International Convention on Oil Pollution Preparedness, Response and Co-operation. It ratified the 1992 IMO Protocols on civil liability and compensation for oil pollution of the sea in 1998; steps are being taken to ratify the HNS Convention on liability for risks caused by chemicals and LPG.

3. Nature Protection

Protection of marine mammals

Celtic seas contain over 36 000 harbour porpoises, 75 000 common dolphins and a large number of grey seals. The seal population is said to damage fisheries and aquaculture. *Protection of whales, porpoises and dolphins* was strengthened in 1991 with the creation of a sanctuary extending 200 miles from the coast where hunting of these animals is totally banned. Ireland was the first country to establish a sanctuary for such protected species throughout its fishery zone. Prohibition of driftnets for tuna fishing as from 2002, under EU regulation, will have positive effects in regard to dolphin by-catch. Total Allowable Catches (TACs) have been lowered for the Irish Sea, where cod stocks are below safe biological limits and other stocks such as haddock, whiting and prawns are severely depleted.

Protected natural areas

Ireland's protected areas programme, which began to expand in the early 1980s, aims to *conserve biodiversity in 10% of its territory*. Areas set aside for nature conservation include national parks and nature reserves (0.9% of the territory). *Five national parks* have management plans; a sixth (10 000 hectares in North Mayo) was acquired in 1998. Designated Natural Heritage Areas (NHAs) where economic activities may also take place cover more than 10% of the territory and are mostly privately owned (Table 7.2).

Special Areas of Conservation (SACs) were selected among the list of NHAs in response to the 1992 Habitat directive. Because the Irish Regulations date to 1997, only a fraction of the 400 proposed SACs have so far been notified to the EU. Under the Irish Constitution, owners who suffer income losses as a consequence of such designation are eligible for compensation. They need to receive formal notice in order to be able to object to a designation, and this may only be done on scientific grounds. Owners affected by SAC designation may also benefit from agri-environmental payments under the REPS scheme (IEP 20 million per year).

Table 7.2 **Categories of protected areas,** 1998

Category	Number	Area (ha)	Comments
National parks	5	47 287	Conservation of flora and fauna and habitats – State ownership
Nature reserves	78	18 095	Nature conservation and public use and appreciation – State ownership
Special Protection Areas (SPAs)	109	230 000	Conservation of bird species and habitats of European importance – statutory protection
Special Areas of Conservation (SACs)*a*	400	650 000	Conservation of fauna, flora and habitats of European importance – statutory protection
Natural Heritage Areas (NHAs)	1 100	750 000	Protection of fauna, flora, habitats and geological sites of national importance – no statutory protection pending new legislation
Ramsar sites	47	70 550	Conservation of wetlands of international importance under Ramsar Convention – State ownership or statutory protection
Biosphere reserves	2	11 500	Nature conservation and sustainable use – UNESCO – State ownership or statutory protection
Biogenetic reserves	14	6 587	Conservation of biodiversity in sites recognised by Council of Europe –State ownership or protected as nature reserves
World Heritage Sites	2	803	Conservation of sites or features of global environmental and/or heritage value recognised by UNESCO

a) Proposal.
Source: DAHGI.

Special Protection Areas (SPAs) were introduced in response to the EU Birds directive and, like the SACs, benefit from the 1997 Regulations. The number of *Ramsar sites* recently increased from 20 to 47; they are located in nature reserves, national parks or SPAs.

Protected areas are under *pressure from agricultural development* stimulated by the Common Agricultural Policy. Between 1975 and 1991, 500 000 hectares was drained or reclaimed under various EU-assisted schemes. Overgrazing is a threat in certain counties. Under the effect of EU agricultural subsidies, the number of sheep increased from 3.3 million in 1980 to 8.9 million in 1992 (7.7 million in 1997). Water pollution by nutrients and pesticides is increasing. To overcome these problems, the *Rural Environment Protection Scheme (REPS)* has been put in place in accordance with the 1992 CAP reform (agri-environmental accompanying measures) (Table 5.4). It should reach 30% of all farmers by 2000, helping to protect Ireland's unique landscapes.

Peatlands

According to the 1990 Environment Action Programme, "Irish peatlands are unique in European terms but are in serious danger due to various types of development". *Peat bogs* once covered 1.3 million hectares (16% of total land area); only 220 000 hectares (3% of land area) remains in its *original condition.*

Peatlands continue to be *threatened by large-scale extraction* for fuel and horticultural peat, afforestation programmes, intensification of agriculture and land reclamation. Active raised bogs are most threatened by mechanical peat extraction; blanket bogs are threatened by sheep overgrazing as well. The importance of conserving Irish peatlands has been recognised at international level by the Council of Europe, the European Parliament and the EU.

A very small part of these peatlands (40 000 hectares) is *fully protected* through government ownership as National Nature Reserves or National Parks. Approximately 200 000 hectares of blanket bogs, heath and upland, and 8 000 hectares of raised bogs, were proposed as candidate SACs in 1997. Negotiations with bog owners and users are under way to ensure long-term conservation; limited compensation has been made available. Conservation policies for peatlands are not yet harmonised with energy (peat burning), agriculture and social (unemployment in deprived areas) policies.

Biological diversity

Owing to Ireland's location, and to agricultural practices going back centuries, *Irish fauna* is not very extensive. Seven vertebrate species are extinct, 12 endangered, six vulnerable, 16 rare and eight indeterminate. Ireland ratified the Convention on Biological Diversity in 1996 and issued its first national report on implementation in 1998. A National Biodiversity Plan is currently in preparation; a preliminary draft was circulated to the main government departments involved with biodiversity, as a basis for discussion. Comments and submissions were also requested from NGOs and the public.

4.   Transfrontier Air Pollution

Sulphur oxides

Among western European countries, Ireland is a *relatively large emitter of SO_2*. On a per capita basis, it emits 49 kg; this is above the OECD Europe average (30 kg) and higher than in most EU countries. On a GDP basis, it emits 2.5 kg/USD 1 000; this, too, is above the OECD Europe average (2.0 kg/ USD 1 000).

In 1990 Ireland announced in its Environment Action Programme that it would accede to the *Helsinki Protocol*. Sulphur emissions subsequently decreased, and by 1993 the target of a 30% reduction in SO_2 emissions was nearly reached. However, "on economic competitiveness grounds" it did not sign the Helsinki Protocol. In 1994 it signed the *Oslo Protocol*, under which it was to achieve a 30% reduction in 2000 (maximum SO_2 emissions of 155 000 tonnes). Since 1993, SO_2 emissions have exceeded this level every year except in 1996. In 1998 the amount was 180 000 tonnes. Meeting the 2000 target requires significant measures, which are set out in a voluntary agreement with the electricity sector (a decrease in SO_2 emission of 40 000 tonnes, mostly during the year 2000).

Concerning *actions planned and taken*, the Environment Action Programme stated that, to meet the 155 000 tonne limit, the following steps would be taken individually or in combination: use of low-sulphur coal at the Moneypoint power station; continued use of natural gas by electricity companies; installation, if necessary, of desulphurisation equipment at electric power stations; and substantial reduction of SO_2 emissions from industrial sources. Between 1990 and 1998, SO_2 emissions from the electricity generation sector increased from 103 000 to 111 500 tonnes. SO_2 emissions from large combustion plants nevertheless remained within the limit set by the EU directive on these plants (124 kt). In 1999, the measures planned in 1990 relating to Moneypoint and other electric power stations had only been partially implemented. Coal-fired stations are not yet subject to integrated pollution control (scheduled for 2001/2002). However, a voluntary agreement with ESB aims to reduce SO_x emissions in 2000 through greater use of low-sulphur coal and oil (less than 1% in 2003).

At the end of 1999, Ireland signed the *Gothenburg Protocol* on abatement of acidification, eutrophication and ground level ozone, which provides a new, very strict SO_2 emission target of 42 000 tonnes by 2010. This will require adoption of very strict measures on all fuels.

Nitrogen oxides

Ireland is a *relatively small emitter of NO$_x$*. On a per capita basis, it emits 33.9 kg, more than the OECD Europe average (28.2 kg). Emissions on a GDP basis are near the OECD Europe average. A programme for retrofitting burners at electric power stations, begun in 1992, considerably reduced NO_x emissions.

As a party to the *Sofia Protocol*, Ireland should have capped its NO_x emissions from 1994 at the 1987 level of 105 000 tonnes. They have always exceeded this limit and have slowly increased since 1995. While the NO_x emissions limit for large combustion plants (50 000 tonnes) has been met, rapid transport sector growth since 1994 explains why Ireland is in breach of the Sofia Protocol. Further measures are needed in regard to both the energy and transport sectors.

Under the 1999 *Gothenburg Protocol*, NO_x emissions (125 000 tonnes in 1998) should be reduced to 65 000 tonnes in 2010. This new target constitutes a very significant challenge for Ireland.

Volatile organic compounds

Ireland is the only EU country that did not sign the VOCs Protocol, stating that this was "due to lack of robust inventories". Therefore, it is not bound to reduce emissions by 30% by 1999 (compared to 1990 levels). *VOCs emissions* (excluding solvents) fell between 1990 and 1994 and have increased since, mostly as a result of transport sector growth. On the whole, there was an increase in VOCs emissions between 1990 and 1998. Once EU legislation concerning vehicles, petrol storage and solvents is implemented, these emissions should be reduced; under the 1999 Gothenburg Protocol, they should fall from the 1998 level of 117 000 tonnes to 55 000 tonnes by 2010.

Long-range transport of air pollutants

There is relatively little acid deposition in Ireland. Foreign sources represent 66% of SO_2 and 85% of NO_x deposition (Table 7.4). With its relatively small population and favourable industry mix, Ireland's contribution to acidification in Europe is insignificant.

5. Climate Change

Climate change is very high on the Irish Government's environmental agenda and is of concern to the Irish population. Expected effects of climate change are increased agricultural and forestry production, more frequent winter flooding, reduced summer recharge of aquifers, possible loss of peatlands, and damage to coastal areas due to sea level rise and greater storminess.

Actions and results in the 1990s

Ireland's greenhouse gas emissions are about 0.1% of the world total. In 1998, they included CO_2 (63%), CH_4 (21%) and N_2O (17%). CO_2 emissions are mainly generated by combustion of fossil fuels and peat (95%); CH_4 emissions mainly from agriculture and waste, and N_2O emissions mainly from agriculture (Table 7.3). As a whole, *agriculture generates 32.5% of GHG emissions*, a larger share than in most OECD countries. *CO_2 emissions are below the OECD average* on a per capita and per unit of GDP basis. Energy intensity is below the OECD average, and the fall in energy intensity between 1980 and 1997 was much greater than the OECD average. Emissions of CH_4 and N_2O per capita are very high compared with most other OECD countries because of the importance of agriculture.

In 1993, Ireland adopted a *national CO_2 emissions abatement strategy* with the goal of *limiting growth of gross CO_2 emissions to 20% by 2000*, taking into account increased sink capacity. A series of measures were taken in the 1990s to mitigate GHG emissions across all sectors, including:

- intensification of energy efficiency and conservation programmes;
- better insulation of buildings;
- improving transportation efficiency;
- accelerating afforestation;
- reducing fertiliser use in agriculture;
- improving the fiscal regime concerning cars, parking and greater use of public transport.

As a result of such measures, growth of CO_2 emissions has been less than that of energy consumption. However, current projections show that the national *20% growth limit for CO_2 will be exceeded* in 2000: CO_2 emissions are expected to be 34% above 1990 levels. Net GHG emissions in 1998 were 17% above 1990. The discrepancy between these emissions and the targeted reduction is partly explained by the fact that in 1993 the subsequent annual economic growth of 9% was not foreseen.

Recent commitments and planned actions

Under the UN Framework Convention on Climate Change, the EU committed itself to stabilise CO_2 emissions by 2000 at their 1990 level. In 1997, it agreed in the Kyoto Protocol to reduce GHG emissions by 8% relative to 1990 levels

Table 7.3 **Greenhouse gas emissions,** 1998

(kt)

	CO_2	CH_4	N_2O	Other
Energy	37 707	49	4.5	–
Industrial processes	2 250	–	2.6	–
Agriculture	–	564	25.3	–
Land use change and forestry	–6 448	–	–	–
Waste	–	76	–	
Total (kt)[a]	40 019	689	32.5	256
Relative weight[b]	(62.6%)	(21.3%)	(15.7%)	(0.4%)

a) Emissions only; sink excluded.
b) In CO_2 equivalent.
Source: EPA, 2000.

Table 7.4 **Deposition of SO_2 and NO_x,** 1996

(100 tonnes)

	SO_2		NO_x	
	Deposition from emissions in Ireland	Deposition in Ireland from other countries	Deposition from emissions in Ireland	Deposition in Ireland from other countries
Ireland	98	98 (34%)	22	22 (15%)
United Kingdom	45	113	23	65
Germany	5	25	5	20
France	9	11	6	15
Other EU countries	5	7	6	13
Non-EU countries	5	31	5	13
Sub-total	69	187 (66%)	45	126 (85%)
Total	167	285	67	148

Source: EMEP.

by 2008-12. Ireland's target under the EU burden sharing agreement is to *limit growth of GHG emissions to 13% above 1990 levels* by 2008-12. National projections show that, under the business as usual scenario, the CO_2 emissions level in 2010 might be 63% above the 1990 level and the GHG emissions level 37% above 1990.

© OECD 2000

Ireland prepared two national communications to the Conference of the Parties. It also commissioned various studies to outline possible *options to meet its international CO_2 and GHG commitments*. One report identified measures providing economic benefits, such as replacement of coal- and oil-fired power stations and peat plants by combined cycle gas turbines, and increased efficiency improvements in the transport sector. It also concluded that a carbon tax could have a positive effect on the Irish economy, provided other taxes were reduced.

In September 1999, the Department of Public Enterprise issued a *Green Paper on Sustainable Energy* establishing a new framework for energy efficiency and use of renewable energy sources. It received the full backing of the Government. The Green Paper complements the *National Abatement Strategy for Greenhouse Gases*, which was to have been published at the end of 1999 by the Department of the Environment and Local Government. It clearly sets out the benefits of best available technology for new power plants, while recognising the benefits of delaying actions in respect of existing plants to the period 2000-08 "unless international arrangements give credit for early action". Fuel switching (i.e. from oil to natural gas) nevertheless needs to take place before 2005, when Ireland is to report on demonstrable progress in achieving the Kyoto targets. However, various constraints must be taken into account in planning and implementing a policy of fuel switching. The National Abatement Strategy will likely include various measures such as switching from coal and oil to gas, improving peat conversion efficiency, increasing the price of domestic heating, improving insulation of buildings, higher energy charges or taxes, petrol and diesel charges, disincentives for large cars, removal of energy subsidies, emission trading, further afforestation and continued development of renewable energy.

Assessment of future results and strategic issues

When the National Abatement Strategy is adopted, it will be possible to assess the extent to which the *GHG target for 2008-12* is likely to be met, taking into account economic growth (which is assumed to vary from the current 8% per year to 4% in 2010) as well as reduced EU funding. A GHG strategy needs to recognise that Ireland has little hydropower and an isolated electricity grid, and that it has decided not to use nuclear energy. Moreover, Irish industry has low energy inefficiency. There is also some reluctance to take measures that would affect the farming community or general public. In this context, it is not surprising that electricity prices in Ireland are lower than those in western Europe (Table 3.2) and that transport fuel prices are lower than in Northern Ireland (Table 6.3). Energy prices could therefore be increased without undue hardship.

With expected economic growth, it is foreseen that under the business as usual scenario net CO_2 emissions would grow by 63% between 1990 and 2010, while CH_4 emissions would fall by 5% and N_2O emissions would increase by 7%. The reduction in GHG emissions introduced by the planned expansion of the forest sink by 2010 should be around 3%. Unless additional measures are taken, CO_2 emissions could increase by 63% between 1990 and 2010 because of growth occurring in the transport (+ 180%), tertiary (+ 68%), electricity (+ 62%), process (+ 67%) and industry (+ 41%) sectors.

Peat is a subsidised energy source that emits a high level of CO2 per unit of energy (1.6 kg CO2/kWh electricity, compared with 0.5 kg CO2 for a single cycle gas-fuelled power station) as well as other pollutants, and whose extraction is environmentally damaging. There is great reluctance to downsize the peat industry through elimination of subsidies, as it is a major employer in midland and western areas (2 000 jobs). Peat energy currently accounts for 7% of TPES. It is foreseen that peat use for electricity production will increase from 0.52 million toe in 1998 to 0.65 million toe in 2005 and then decrease (to 0.50 million toe in 2010). Peat-related CO2 emissions have been estimated at 2.5 Mt in 1998, 3.16 Mt in 2005 and 2.4 Mt in 2010. A new peat-fired electric power station (IEP 100 million) will start operating at the end of 2000. One-fifth of the capital cost is supported by a EU grant. Some old plants are due to close in the next few years, to be replaced by more fuel efficient ones. The OECD-IEA has estimated the producer subsidy equivalent for peat production in 1997-98 at IEP 5 per tonne, i.e. IEP 15 million per year or IEP 12 226 per employee year. A consultant report suggests that replacing peat use in power stations with combined cycle gas turbines would have economic benefits and reduce CO2 emissions and damage to the landscape; the economic benefits should cover the costs of social measures to alleviate unemployment. Closure could be restricted to the 11 peat plants built in the 1950s and 1960s, with the more efficient plants under construction continuing to operate.

6. Other Global Issues

Follow-up to UNCED

In 1995, Ireland issued guidelines to promote preparation of *local Agenda 21s* by counties and other local authorities. County Councils and boroughs have designated local Agenda 21 officers, who are networked at regional and national levels. This provides a forum for exchanging experience and examples of good practice. So far, very few local Agenda 21s have been prepared. Committees set up for this purpose are not always consulted on local issues with potentially severe environmental consequences.

Ozone depleting substances (ODS)

Ireland *does not produce CFCs or other ODS*. Under essential uses provisions, it imports less than 700 tonnes of CFCs per year for manufacturing inhalers, most of which are subsequently exported. Such import is being phased out as non-CFC inhalers are approved. Ireland also imports 40-50 tonnes of methyl bromide for use as a soil fumigant. Implementation of international ODS agreements is carried out based on the 1994 EU regulation, which will be replaced by a new one incorporating the latest Montreal Protocol amendments.

Activities aimed at *collecting, recycling or destroying existing CFCs or halons* are very limited. It is illegal to release CFCs, or to accept a refrigerator containing them at a waste dump, but no illegal venting of CFCs or halons has yet been prosecuted.

International trade and investment

Ireland has attracted a large number of enterprises in the manufacturing sector. It ranks first among OECD countries in terms of its share of foreign affiliates in gross manufacturing output and its share of employment in foreign affiliates. It has attracted a *large number of multinational chemical and pharmaceutical factories*. These are very modern and meet strict environmental requirements. Various environmental issues relating to chemicals are being addressed by a number of government departments. An ad hoc group was recently set up to streamline national chemicals policy. This would include, in particular, better implementation of relevant OECD Council Acts where they have not already been transposed under EU legislation.

Most of Ireland's *hazardous waste* is managed internally. About 15% is exported, mostly to western Europe for thermal treatment. During the 1990s, when the United Kingdom decided to limit imports of foreign waste for disposal in landfills, Ireland had to reduce its waste exports.

Ireland has been controlling import and export of *endangered species* through the relevant EU Regulation. Ratification of the 1973 Washington Convention (CITES) awaits adoption of an amendment to the 1976 Wildlife Act which would enable public authorities to exercise better enforcement.

At USD 10 per capita, well above the OECD average (USD 5.1 per capita), Ireland is a relatively large importer of *tropical woods*. In 1994, out of 70 000 tonnes, most came from Ghana and Côte d'Ivoire. Ratification of the 1994 International Tropical Timber Agreement is expected in the near future.

Ireland participates in WTO discussions on *environment and trade*. It favours Multilateral Environmental Agreements and considers that the precautionary principle should be introduced in WTO procedures.

Figure 7.1   **Official development assistance, 1998**[a]

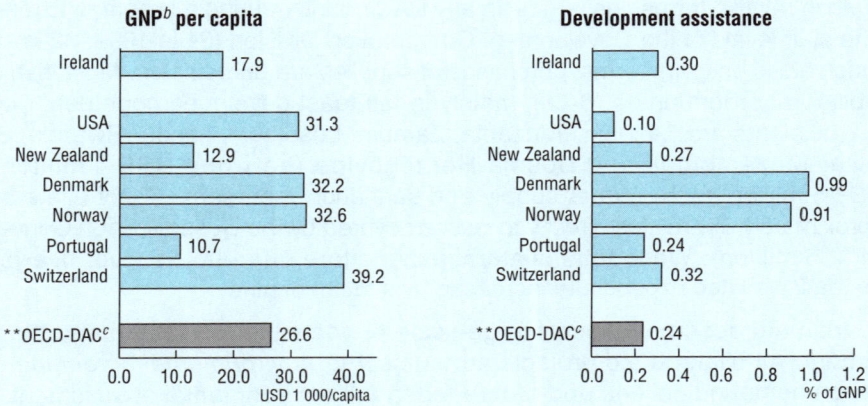

GNP[b] per capita	Development assistance

a) Provisional data.
b) GNP in USD at current exchange rates.
c) Member countries of the OECD Development Assistance Committee.
Source: OECD-DAC.

Development assistance

The purpose of *Irish development assistance* is to work towards "the overall goal of international peace, security and a just and stable global economic system". Policy objectives include promoting sustainable development, fostering environmental protection, supporting sustainable growth and development, and assisting sustainable development of the world's poorest countries.

In 1992, Irish official development aid amounted to 0.16% of GNP. The Government then pledged to increase ODA to 0.20% in 1993, and by 0.05% each year thereafter. The target was met in 1993, 1994 and 1995. In 1997, projected aid was IEP 135 million (0.40% GNP) and the actual amount was IEP 124 million (0.31% GNP). In 1998, the target for 1997 was achieved (IEP 139.6 million). As a whole, Irish aid in 1998 represented 0.30% of GNP, a value well above that for DAC (Figure 7.1). However, this was below the DAC average country effort (0.40%) and the EU average (0.33%). The projected level of Irish aid in 1999 is *0.35% of GNP*. A Cabinet level agreement has been worked out, with a commitment on budgetary allocations for three years (1999-2001). An increase to *0.45% in 2002* is currently projected, with the UN goal of 0.7% of GNP being achieved eventually.

Between 1992 and 1998, *aid increased* from USD 70 million to 199 million. This growth in relative terms, the largest in any DAC country during this period, is reflected in the staff levels of the Development Co-operation Division (31 in 1992, 82 in 1999). All Irish aid is on grant terms; purchases of supplies are unrestricted. Most Irish aid is for bilateral programmes (64%), mainly in the least developed countries. The top nine recipients are Ethiopia, Tanzania, Zambia, Lesotho, Uganda, Rwanda, South Africa, Mozambique and Bosnia-Herzegovina (between USD 4 million and USD 15 million each). Water supply and sanitation represents 7% of bilateral *aid*. Approximately 3% relates directly to issues covered by the Desertification Convention (IEP 2.6 million). While total bilateral expenditure quadrupled (over five years), Agenda 21-related expenditure increased by a factor of nine.

Irish aid does not support large-scale projects that could damage the environment. All bilateral aid projects are subject to *environmental screening* using environmental guidelines and, if needed, a full environmental assessment. Irish multilateral aid (36%) is mostly through the EU (21%), UN agencies (9%) and the World Bank group (4%). In particular, Ireland participates in the GEF (IEP 1.70 million in 1994 to 1997, IEP 3.69 million in 1998-2001). It supports the Multilateral Fund under the Montreal Protocol (Ozone Fund), UNEP, and voluntary contributions to UN Trust Funds (Climate Change, Biodiversity and Desertification Conventions). Ireland also contributes to UNDP and World Bank environmental activities.

7. Environmental Performance

Ireland made considerable progress during the 1990s by transposing and implementing a number of very significant EU directives, and by ratifying and implementing several international environmental protection agreements. In some instances these agreements dated to the 1970s or early 1980s, when Ireland took a less active part in international environmental activities. It is *now a full player* in environmental co-operation at the *EU and global levels*.

Additional *international agreements* could also reasonably be ratified (Annex III). Attention should be given to OECD Council Acts that have not yet been taken into account through EU legislation, notably those relating to chemicals, hazardous waste, pollutant releases and environmental information.

European and bilateral co-operation

Ireland stands out among EU countries for its rapid transposition of EU directives. It is the EU cohesion country which received *the largest EU financial support*, and the one with the most rapid economic growth during the late 1990s. The large amount of spending on environmental infrastructure that has been initiated should provide improved environmental protection in years to come.

Most environmental investment, however, is still to come and may depend increasingly on national funding. Financing the operational costs of new water infrastructure is likely to create budgetary difficulties unless there is a separate charging mechanism for households (User-Pays Principle). Like other EU countries, Ireland has had difficulties implementing a number of directives (e.g. drinking water, urban waste water, habitat, EIA).

Ireland co-operates with Northern Ireland on a number of local transfrontier issues. This co-operation between local authorities, supported by EU funds, has produced concrete results such as the All Island chemical waste management system. More progress can be foreseen with the entry into force of the Good Friday Agreement. At the end of 1999, the North/South Ministerial Council agreed upon a programme of work and arrangements for enhanced co-operation, including in the field of environment. Ireland co-operates with the United Kingdom, particularly Wales and the Isle of Man, on a number of marine pollution issues involving the Irish Sea. It is very concerned about release of radioactive substances in the marine environment, as well as the appearance on its coasts of ammunition dumped in the Irish Sea after the Second World War. Good co-operation with the UK on these issues has led to a better appreciation of the situation. Ireland continues to press for closure of the UK's Sellafield nuclear reprocessing plant.

Commitments concerning marine environment

Protecting the marine environment is very important in Ireland, where over 60% of the population lives in coastal areas which are under intense pressure from growing urbanisation, tourism and aquaculture as well as sea fishing, offshore gas and oil exploitation and maritime transport. Irish beaches are very clean overall and bathing water quality is high. Nonetheless, some areas are still polluted by discharges of untreated sewage water from land-based sources. Progress towards eliminating such pollution will be achieved when the waste water treatment plants under construction begin operating.

Ireland has taken strict measures to protect the sea mammals in its waters, and to ban incineration and dumping of harmful substances at sea. Progress has also been made concerning surveillance of ships carrying nuclear or hazardous cargoes in the Irish Sea, with prior notification of passage being increasingly carried out. Preparedness for oil pollution emergencies has been strengthened, and foreign assistance has been secured in case of a large oil spill. Dumping and incineration activities are banned or under very strict control.

Commitments concerning biodiversity and nature protection

In the 1980s, Ireland took positive steps to protect its valuable biodiversity. Considerable progress was achieved in the 1990s, especially relating to protected areas covered by international agreements or EU legislation: protected areas currently cover *7% of the territory*. National Parks expanded from 21 000 hectares in 1983 to 47 000 hectares in 1997. A sixth national park (North Mayo) was created in 1998.

Nature reserves could be enlarged in number and size. Special attention should be paid to Ireland's *peat bogs*, which are unique in western Europe and attract many tourists. Destruction of these bogs, which are so much a part of the country's heritage, as a result of energy subsidies is an issue requiring greater attention. Progress on nature protection has been slow due to *lack of resources* for conservation activities or for compensation of property owners. *Nature protection legislation is pending*: so far, neither the amendment to the 1976 Wildlife Act nor the National Park Act has been adopted. In the meantime, degradation of unprotected natural habitats has continued. Special protection areas for birds (relating to the EU bird directive) are now quite significant, but the EU undertook two infringement procedures against Ireland before it obtained this result. Four hundred special areas of conservation (relating to the habitat directive) have been identified, but only some have been notified to the European Commission as the lengthy designation procedure only began in 1997. Ireland's *Biological Diversity Strategy* has not been finalised. Ratification of the 1973 Washington Convention (CITES) is still pending.

Commitments concerning air pollution

To reduce *acid deposition*, which mostly originates beyond its borders and has not reached a high level, Ireland needs to enter into agreement with other countries and to meet its own commitments. So far, it has made international commitments on SO_2, NO_x and VOCs. During the 1990s measures were taken to reduce SO_2 emissions, notably from industrial sources; these emissions are higher than the OECD average.

SO_2 emissions in 1998 were about 15% higher than foreseen for 2000 under the *Oslo Protocol*. NO_x emissions per capita are above the OECD Europe average. Despite measures taken, Ireland has not met its commitments to stabilise NO_x emissions under the *Sofia Protocol*. It is the only EU country which did not sign the *VOCs Protocol*; emissions of VOCs increased between 1990 and 1998. Due to limited progress controlling emissions regulated under UN-ECE protocols, Ireland needs to make a *much greater effort* in years to come in order to meet the targets established for 2010 under the new Gothenburg Protocol. Admittedly, by that time all *power stations* will use BATNEEC and their emissions will be considerably reduced.

Climate change

The Irish Government takes climate change very seriously. Having undertaken the necessary studies, it adopted a strategy to reduce CO_2 emissions in 1993 and has already implemented a number of measures. It did not meet its *national 1993 commitment* to limit CO_2 growth by 2000 to 20% above 1990 levels, to a certain extent because of strong economic growth between 1994 and 1999, but also partly because mandatory and pricing measures to better control CO_2 emissions were not introduced during this period. In view of the accumulated data and other information on implementing an effective climate change policy at the Government's disposal, it should soon be in a position to announce effective measures enabling Ireland to achieve its Kyoto emissions target for 2010.

Significant efforts must be made in this area, as there is a *need to reduce emissions more than 20% over ten years* compared with the business as usual scenario. Such reduction will require initiatives by the power generation industry and taking of measures that have been postponed for many years: increases in the prices of energy, electricity, petrol and diesel fuel, as well as drastic reduction of fossil fuel use. Price increases should be designed to produce a decrease in CO_2 emissions with limited social effects, especially on poor families, and limited economic effects, using in particular offset mechanisms for generation and transport. As similar measures will be taken by other EU countries, the competitiveness margin of Irish exporters would not be significantly affected. Mandatory measures or targets will be required, as well as economic or fiscal measures and awareness raising and information dissemination.

Sustainable development

Implementation of a climate change strategy could provide an opportunity for the Government to demonstrate that it can carry out a policy of *sustainable development during an economic boom*. In particular, this could affect the extent to which peat should continue to be used as fuel, considering its economic subsidisation and negative environmental effects (landscape damage, emissions of air pollutants).

Ireland has elaborated a Strategy on Sustainable Development and taken steps to launch the local Agenda 21 process. *Progress has been slow*, but should lead to useful results. In response to the Rio Declaration, there have been very substantial public participation activities and wide consultation with social partners and NGOs. This policy should be continued in regard to present and future international commitments, particularly the Aarhus Convention and the OECD Recommendation on environmental information.

Environmental aid

Ireland is the DAC country whose official development assistance has increased the most since 1992. Its *level of ODA is now in line with the EU average* and is projected to be 0.45% in 2002. Ireland is therefore moving towards the target of 0.7% GNP endorsed at Rio. Furthermore, it is providing new and additional resources in support of environmental activities. Promoting sustainable development and environmental protection are among the purposes of Irish development aid; related expenditures exceed 15% of the total. As Irish aid is not very large in absolute terms, it is focused on Africa's least developed countries. In its priority countries programmes, the proportion of expenditure allocated to supporting environmental protection increased between 1993 and 1996 from 18 to 36% of the total.

ANNEXES

Annex I: Selected Environmental Data[1]

	IRL	CAN	MEX	USA	JPN	KOR	AUS	NZL	AUT	BEL	CZE	DN
LAND												
Total area (1 000 km²)	**70**	9 971	1 958	9 364	378	99	7 713	270	84	31	79	43
Major protected areas (% of total area)[2]	**0.9**	9.6	8.2	21.2	6.8	6.9	7.7	23.5	29.2	2.8	16.2	32.6
Nitrogenous fertiliser use (t/km² of arable land)	**43.2**	4.1	4.4	6.2	11.5	23.1	1.7	37.3	7.6	18.8	6.8	12.3
FOREST												
Forest area (% of land area)	**8.8**	45.3	33.4	32.6	66.8	65.2	19.4	29.5	47.6	22.2	34.1	10.5
Use of forest resources (harvest/growth)	**0.6**	0.4	0.2	0.6	0.3	0.1	..	0.6	0.6	0.9	0.7	0.6
Tropical wood imports (USD/cap.)[3]	**10.1**	0.8	0.1	1.6	18.4	11.1	4.6	2.6	0.2	12.3	0.1	4.4
THREATENED SPECIES												
Mammals (% of species known)	**6.5**	19.2	33.2	10.5	7.7	17.0	14.9	15.2	35.4	31.6	33.3	24.0
Birds (% of species known)	**21.8**	10.8	16.9	7.2	8.3	15.0	6.4	25.3	37.0	27.5	66.1	10.6
Fish (% of species known)	**33.3**	6.4	5.7	2.4	11.1	1.3	0.4	0.8	65.5	54.3	29.2	18.2
WATER												
Water withdrawal (% of gross annual availability)	**2.6**	1.7	17.4	19.9	20.8	35.6	4.3	0.6	2.7	42.5	15.6	15.7
Fish catches (% of world catches)	**0.3**	1.0	1.6	5.4	6.3	2.4	0.2	0.6	–	–	–	2.0
Public waste water treatment (% of population served)	**61**	78	22	71	55	53	..	80	75	27	59	87
AIR												
Emissions of sulphur oxides (kg/cap.)	**48.7**	89.7	24.4	69.3	7.2	32.9	100.6	12.3	7.1	23.6	68.0	20.7
" (kg/1 000 USD GDP)[4]	**2.5**	4.3	3.9	2.5	0.4	2.9	5.2	0.8	0.4	1.3	6.2	1.0
Emissions of nitrogen oxides (kg/cap.)	**33.9**	67.8	17.2	80.2	11.3	27.6	118.3	45.9	21.3	32.8	41.1	46.9
" (kg/1 000 USD GDP)[4]	**1.8**	3.4	2.8	2.9	0.6	2.5	6.1	3.1	1.1	1.8	3.8	2.2
Emissions of carbon dioxide (t./cap.)[5]	**10.3**	15.9	3.7	20.5	9.3	9.2	16.5	8.8	7.9	12.0	11.7	11.8
" (t./1 000 USD GDP)[4]	**0.58**	0.77	0.60	0.75	0.45	0.78	0.83	0.59	0.42	0.63	1.08	0.56
WASTE GENERATED												
Industrial waste (kg/1 000 USD GDP)[4,6]	**78**	..	60	..	57	71	119	33	75	74	345	25
Municipal waste (kg/cap.)[7]	**560**	500	310	720	400	400	690	350	510	480	310	560
Nuclear waste (t./Mtoe of TPES)[8]	**–**	5.6	0.3	1.0	1.9	2.1	–	–	–	1.4	1.1	–
NOISE												
Population exposed to leq>65dB(A) (million inh.)[9]	**..**	..	..	17.2	38.0	..	..	..	1.2	1.2	1.5	0.5

.. Not available.
– Nil or negligible.
* Figures in italics include: for Germany: western Germany only;
  for United Kingdom: threatened species: Great Britain only.
  water withdrawal and public waste water treatment: England and Wales only.
a) Data for Luxembourg are included under Belgium.
1. Data refer to the latest available year. They include provisional figures and Secretariat estimates. Partial totals are underlined.
   Varying definitions can limit comparability across countries.
2. Data refer to IUCN categories I to VI; AUS, HUN, TUR: national data.
Source: OECD Environmental Data, Compendium 1999.

Annex I: ***Selected Environmental Data[1]***

FIN	FRA	DEU*	GRC	HUN	ISL	ITA	LUX	NLD	NOR	POL	PRT	ESP	SWE	CHE	TUR	UKD*	OECD*
338	549	357	132	93	103	301	3	42	324	313	92	506	450	41	779	245	34 728
8.4	10.1	26.9	2.6	9.1	9.5	7.3	6.5	11.6	24.2	9.4	6.6	8.4	8.1	18.0	3.8	20.4	12.6
7.1	13.4	14.8	7.8	5.4	8.9	8.4	a	37.7	12.3	6.1	4.0	5.4	7.3	12.8	4.3	19.5	6.4
75.5	31.4	30.1	22.8	18.9	1.3	23.3	34.4	9.2	39.2	29.7	37.9	32.3	73.5	31.7	26.9	10.5	33.8
0.8	0.7	0.4	0.6	0.6	–	0.3	0.5	0.6	0.4	0.6	0.8	0.5	0.7	0.5	0.4	0.7	0.6
1.9	7.1	2.0	3.4	0.1	4.0	6.6	a	17.3	4.5	0.2	19.9	6.2	2.0	0.5	0.9	3.3	5.1
11.9	20.2	36.7	37.9	71.1	–	32.2	51.6	15.6	5.9	15.5	17.3	21.2	18.2	34.2	22.2	22.2	..
6.7	14.3	29.2	13.0	18.8	13.3	24.7	50.0	27.1	6.3	16.6	13.7	14.1	8.6	42.6	6.7	6.8	..
11.9	6.6	68.2	24.3	32.1	–	..	27.9	82.1	–	27.1	18.6	29.4	12.7	44.7	9.9	11.1	..
2.2	23.9	24.4	12.1	5.0	0.1	32.2	3.4	4.9	0.7	18.7	11.9	36.8	1.5	4.9	15.2	14.6	11.8
0.2	0.6	0.3	0.2	–	2.4	0.4	–	0.5	3.1	0.4	0.2	1.2	0.4	–	0.5	1.0	30.9
77	77	89	45	22	4	61	88	97	67	47	21	48	93	94	12	88	59
19.5	16.2	15.8	48.3	64.7	32.1	23.1	8.4	8.0	6.9	61.3	36.2	49.1	10.3	4.6	29.8	34.5	39.2
1.1	0.9	0.8	4.6	8.0	1.7	1.3	0.2	0.4	0.3	10.8	3.3	3.5	0.6	0.2	5.2	2.0	2.2
50.5	29.1	21.7	35.2	19.4	105.6	30.9	39.6	28.5	50.6	29.9	37.6	31.7	38.1	18.2	14.5	35.0	40.6
2.9	1.5	1.2	3.3	2.4	5.4	1.7	1.2	1.5	2.2	5.2	3.4	2.3	2.1	0.8	2.5	2.0	2.3
12.5	6.2	10.8	7.7	5.7	8.9	7.4	20.5	11.8	7.8	9.1	5.2	6.5	6.0	6.3	2.9	9.4	11.2
0.71	0.32	0.59	0.72	0.71	0.46	0.40	0.62	0.61	0.34	1.49	0.44	0.44	0.33	0.29	0.51	0.52	0.62
139	92	45	60	86	2	21	149	30	30	94	4	26	97	10	94	57	81
410	590	460	370	490	550	460	590	560	630	320	380	390	360	600	330	480	500
2.1	4.6	1.3	–	2.2	–	–	–	0.2	–	..	–	1.8	4.6	2.4	–	3.6	1.6
0.2	9.4	9.5	2.0	..	..	..	..	0.6	0.5	..	3.0	8.9	0.3	0.8	..	5.7	124.0

3.Total imports of cork and wood from non-OECD tropical countries.
4.GDP at 1991 prices and purchasing power parities.
5.CO$_2$ from energy use only; international marine bunkers are excluded.
6.Waste from manufacturing industries.
7.NZL: household waste only.
8.Waste from spent fuel arising in nuclear power plants, in tonnes of heavy metal, per million tonnes of oil equivalent of total primary energy supply.
9.Road traffic noise.

Annex II: Selected Economic Data and Trends[1]

	IRL	CAN	MEX	USA	JPN	KOR	AUS	NZL	AUT	BEL	CZE	DNK
TOTAL AREA (1 000km²)	**70**	9 971	1 958	9 364	378	99	7 713	270	84	31	79	4?
POPULATION												
Total population, 1999 (100 000 inh.)	**37**	305	975	2 713	1 267	469	190	38	81	102	103	5?
% change (1980-1999)	**9.8**	24.2	40.0	19.2	8.2	22.9	29.3	20.3	7.2	3.9	-0.4	3.?
Population density, 1999 (inh./km²)	**53.1**	3.1	49.8	29.0	335.4	471.8	2.5	14.0	96.5	335.0	130.4	123.?
GROSS DOMESTIC PRODUCT[2]												
GDP, 1999 (billion USD)	**77**	666	629	7 936	2 579	553	403	57	161	203	109	11?
% change (1980-1999)	**151.9**	62.4	50.9	77.9	66.9	286.1	88.8	54.1	52.0	42.0	..	52.?
per capita, 1999 (1 000 USD/cap.)	**20.6**	21.8	6.5	29.2	20.4	11.8	21.2	15.1	19.9	19.9	10.6	21.?
INDUSTRY[3]												
Value added in industry (% of GDP)	**39**	27	26	26	37	43	26	26	30	28	37	2?
Industrial production – % change (1980-1998)	**321**	51	60	65	45	382	53	34	65	33	-10	6?
AGRICULTURE												
Value added in agriculture (% of GDP)[4]	**5**	2	6	2	2	6	3	7	1	1	4	4?
ENERGY SUPPLY												
Total supply, 1998 (Mtoe)	**13**	234	148	2 182	510	163	105	17	29	58	41	2?
% change (1980-1998)	**56.2**	21.4	49.5	20.4	47.2	296.2	49.2	85.5	22.9	26.6	-13.2	5.4
Energy intensity, 1998 (Toe/1 000 USD)	**0.19**	0.36	0.24	0.29	0.20	0.32	0.27	0.31	0.18	0.29	0.37	0.18
% change (1980-1998)	**-32.7**	-22.5	2.5	-29.7	-10.6	11.9	-17.9	23.6	-17.4	-9.2	..	-29.9
Structure of energy supply, 1998 (%)[5]												
Solid fuels	**23.3**	16.5	10.0	27.1	18.0	21.6	48.1	10.9	22.3	15.7	52.5	33.7
Oil	**54.9**	34.7	62.3	39.9	51.1	56.2	33.6	38.4	43.4	42.2	20.2	45.2
Gas	**21.2**	28.9	21.3	22.8	11.7	7.6	16.9	24.2	23.3	21.4	18.6	19.9
Nuclear	**–**	7.9	1.6	8.5	17.0	14.3	–	–	–	20.7	8.3	–
Hydro, etc.	**0.7**	12.1	4.7	1.8	2.2	0.2	1.4	26.5	11.1	0.1	0.4	1.2
ROAD TRANSPORT[6]												
Road traffic volumes, 1998 billion veh.-km	**30**	280	54	4 223	772	75	187	29	60	85	31	44
% change (1980-1998)	**62.4**	36.4	27.9	72.9	98.5	763.2	63.3	77.4	70.3	76.5	45.9	67.3
per capita (1 000 veh.-km/cap.)	**8.1**	9.2	0.6	15.7	6.1	1.6	10.0	7.9	7.5	8.3	3.0	8.3
Road vehicle stock, 1998 10 000 vehicles	**138**	1 804	1 389	21 443	7 082	1 047	1 126	216	471	499	377	219
% change (1980-1998)	**71.9**	36.5	138.4	37.6	91.1	1 883.6	55.0	37.8	67.6	43.4	95.3	32.6
per capita (veh./100 inh.)	**37**	60	15	80	56	23	60	58	58	49	37	41

.. Not available.
– Nil or negligible.
* Figures in italics include western Germany only.
Source: OECD Environmental Data, Compendium 1999.

Annex II: Selected Economic Data and Trends[1]

FIN	FRA	DEU*	GRC	HUN	ISL	ITA	LUX	NLD	NOR	POL	PRT	ESP	SWE	CHE	TUR	UKD	OECD*
338	549	357	132	93	103	301	3	42	324	313	92	506	450	41	779	245	34 728
52	591	822	105	101	3	577	4	158	44	387	100	394	89	71	659	594	11 086
8.1	9.7	5.0	9.2	−5.9	20.9	2.2	18.3	11.5	8.8	8.8	1.8	5.5	6.8	11.8	48.3	5.5	15.2
15.3	107.6	230.2	79.8	108.3	2.7	191.5	167.0	380.0	13.7	123.8	108.7	77.9	19.7	172.9	84.6	242.7	31.9
99	1 203	1 564	119	90	6	1 085	15	321	104	255	126	622	171	158	370	1 114	20 908
58.5	44.3	42.0	41.3	..	67.8	38.9	145.6	57.3	70.6	..	66.6	64.5	38.4	28.8	125.0	55.9	66.5
19.1	20.3	19.0	11.3	8.9	21.3	18.8	35.5	20.3	23.4	6.6	12.6	15.8	19.3	22.2	5.6	18.7	18.9
30	26	29	20	32	22	31	21	27	32	39	35	32	27	..	31	28	29
88	21	25	19	14	..	27	61	36	117	..	75	39	61	37	227	34	49
4	2	1	12	7	9	3	1	3	2	8	4	3	2	..	14	2	3
33	256	345	27	25	3	168	3	74	25	96	22	113	52	27	73	233	5 097
31.7	34.5	−4.4	69.0	−12.8	78.8	21.1	−8.9	14.5	35.3	−21.9	112.3	64.4	28.0	27.5	131.6	15.7	25.5
0.35	0.22	0.22	0.23	0.29	0.47	0.16	0.23	0.24	0.25	0.39	0.18	0.19	0.32	0.17	0.19	0.21	0.25
−13.9	−4.5	−31.8	23.5	..	12.9	−11.9	−61.0	−25.0	−20.3	..	31.4	3.6	−3.9	0.4	0.6	−24.5	−22.0
35.5	10.8	25.5	36.8	17.8	2.6	8.2	5.2	13.4	9.3	71.0	19.4	18.6	19.9	5.9	40.1	18.4	23.9
32.9	35.5	40.6	58.8	28.9	31.2	56.9	72.3	37.5	34.0	18.9	72.0	54.7	30.5	49.8	42.0	35.9	41.9
10.2	12.8	21.1	2.7	38.8	−	31.1	22.2	47.6	17.1	9.8	3.2	10.3	1.3	8.7	12.4	34.2	20.6
17.4	38.8	12.2	−	14.4	−	−	−	1.4	−	−	−	13.7	36.2	24.9	−	11.3	10.9
4.0	2.1	0.5	1.7	0.1	66.2	3.8	0.4	0.1	39.5	0.2	5.5	2.7	12.1	10.7	5.5	0.2	2.8
45	491	596	59	27	2	495	4	109	31	128	55	161	73	50	50	454	8 700
67.5	66.0	47.5	187.7	42.6	99.8	118.5	73.0	61.0	63.2	187.2	153.8	127.7	64.2	39.7	237.9	87.7	76.7
8.7	8.3	7.3	5.6	2.7	6.5	8.6	9.0	6.9	7.0	3.3	5.5	4.1	8.2	7.1	0.8	7.7	7.9
231	3 230	4 427	365	273	16	3 433	28	732	221	1 055	425	1 927	415	367	516	2 997	56 468
66.9	48.8	61.0	189.0	132.0	65.3	77.2	93.4	60.5	58.3	244.0	252.7	115.0	34.7	51.1	340.4	72.7	62.4
45	55	54	35	27	58	60	66	47	50	27	43	49	47	52	8	51	51

1. Data may include provisional figures and Secretariat estimates. Partial totals are underlined.
2. GDP at 1991 prices and purchasing power parities.
3. Value added: includes mining and quarrying, manufacturing, gas, electricity and water and construction; HUN, POL: as % of total of branches at basic prices; production: excludes construction; WDEU: % change 1980-1997.
4. Agriculture, forestry, hunting, fishery, etc. HUN, POL: as % of total of branches at basic prices.
5. Breakdown excludes electricity trade.
6. Refers to motor vehicles with four or more wheels, except for Japan and Italy, which include three-wheeled goods vehicles.

Annex III.A: Selected multilateral agreements (worldwide)

Y = in force   S = signed   R = ratified   D = denounced

			CAN	MEX	USA	JPN	KOR	AUS
1946 Washington	Conv. – Regulation of whaling	Y	D	R	R	R	R	R
1956 Washington	Protocol	Y	R	R	R	R	R	R
1949 Geneva	Conv. – Road traffic	Y	R		R	R	R	R
1954 London	Conv. – Prevention of pollution of the sea by oil	Y	R	R	R	R	R	R
1958 Geneva	Conv. – Fishing and conservation of the living resources of the high seas	Y	S	R	R			R
1960 Geneva	Conv. – Protection of workers against ionising radiations (ILO 115)	Y		R		R		
1962 Brussels	Conv. – Liability of operators of nuclear ships							
1963 Vienna	Conv. – Civil liability for nuclear damage	Y		R				
1988 Vienna	Joint protocol relating to the application of the Vienna Convention and the Paris Convention	Y						
1997 Vienna	Protocol to amend the Vienna convention							
1963 Moscow	Treaty – Banning nuclear weapon tests in the atmosphere, in outer space and under water	Y	R	R	R	R	R	R
1964 Copenhagen	Conv. – International council for the exploration of the sea	Y	R		R			
1970 Copenhagen	Protocol	Y	R		R			
1969 Brussels	Conv. – Intervention on the high seas in cases of oil pollution casualties (INTERVENTION)	Y		R	R	R	S	R
1973 London	Protocol (pollution by substances other than oil)	Y		R	R			R
1969 Brussels	Conv. – Civil liability for oil pollution damage (CLC)	Y	R	D	S	D	D	D
1976 London	Protocol	Y	R	R		R	R	R
1992 London	Protocol	Y	R	R		R	R	R
1995 Rome	Code of conduct on responsible fishing							
1970 Bern	Conv. – Transport of goods by rail (CIM)	Y						
1971 Brussels	Conv. – International fund for compensation for oil pollution damage (FUND)	Y	R	D	S	D	D	D
1976 London	Protocol	Y	R	R		R	R	R
1992 London	Protocol	Y	R	R		R	R	R
1971 Brussels	Conv. – Civil liability in maritime carriage of nuclear material	Y						
1971 London, Moscow, Washington	Conv. – Prohib. emplacement of nuclear and mass destruct. weapons on sea-bed, ocean floor and subsoil	Y	R	R	R	R	R	R
1971 Ramsar	Conv. – Wetlands of international importance especially as waterfowl habitat	Y	R	R	R	R		R
1982 Paris	Protocol	Y	R	R	R	R		R
1987 Regina	Regina amendment							
1971 Geneva	Conv. – Protection against hazards of poisoning arising from benzene (ILO 136)	Y						
1972 London, Mexico, Moscow, Washington	Conv. – Prevention of marine pollution by dumping of wastes and other matter (LC)	Y	R	R	R	R	R	R
1996 London	Protocol to the Conv. – Prevention of marine pollution by dumping of wastes and other matter					S		S
1972 Geneva	Conv. – Safe container (CSC)	Y	R	R	R	R	R	R
1972 London, Moscow, Washington	Conv. – International liability for damage caused by space objects	Y	R	R	R	R	R	R
1972 Paris	Conv. – Protection of the world cultural and natural heritage	Y	R	R	R	R	R	R
1973 Washington	Conv. – International trade in endangered species of wild fauna and flora (CITES)	Y	R	R	R	R	R	R
1974 Geneva	Conv. – Prev. and control of occup. hazards caused by carcinog. subst. and agents (ILO 139)	Y			R			
1976 London	Conv. – Limitation of liability for maritime claims (LLMC)	Y		R	R			R

Annex III.A: Selected multilateral agreements (worldwide)

Y = in force   S = signed   R = ratified   D = denounced

NZL	AUT	BEL	CZE	DNK	FIN	FRA	DEU	GRC	HUN	ISL	IRL	ITA	LUX	NLD	NOR	POL	PRT	ESP	SWE	CHE	TUR	UKD	EU
R	R			R	R	R	R			D	**R**	R		R	R			R	R	R			R
R				R		R	R			R	**R**			R	R			R	R	R			R
R	R	R	R	R	R	R		R	R	R	**R**	R	R	R	R	R	R	R	R	S	R	R	R
R	R	R		R	R	R	R	R		R	**R**	R		R	R	R	R	R	R	R			R
S		R		R	R	R				S	**S**			R			R	R		R			R
	R	R	R	R	R	R	R	R			**R**		R	R	R	R	R	R	R	R	R	R	R
	S						S				**S**			R			R						
		R							R							R		S					S
	S	R	R	R	S	S	S	R			**R**		R	R	R	S	S	R	S	S	S		S
		S						S			**S**				S								
R	R	R	R	R	R		R	R	R	R	**R**	R	R	R	R	S	S	R	R	R	R	R	R
		R		R	R	R	R	R		R	**R**			R	R	R	R	R	R				R
		R		R	R	R	R	R		R	**R**			R	R	R	R	R	R				R
R		R		R	R	R	R	S		R	**R**	R		R	R	R	R	R	R	R			R
S		R		R	R	R	R				**R**	R		R	R	R	R	R	R	R			R
R		R		D	D	D	D	D		R	**D**	R	R	D	D	R	R	D	D	D			D
		R		R	R	R	R	R		R	**D**	R	R	R	R	R	R	R	R	R			D
R		R		R	R	R	R	R		R	**R**			R	R	S		R	R	R			R
	R	R	R	R	R	R	R	R	R		**R**	R	R	R	R	R	R	R	R	R	R	R	R
R		R		D	D	D	D	D		R	**D**	R		D	D	R	R	D	D	D		D	
		R		R	R	R	R	R		R	**D**	R		R	R	R	R	R	R				D
R		R		R	R	R	R	R		R	**R**			R	R	S		R	R				R
		R		R	R	R	R							R	R		S	R	R				S
R	R	R	R	R	R			R	R	R	**R**	R	R	R	R	R	R	R	R	R	R	R	R
R	R	R	R	R	R	R	R	R	R	R	**R**	R	S	S	R	R	R	R	R	R	R	R	R
R	R	S	R	R	R	R	R	R	R	R	**R**	R	S	S	R	R	R	R	R	R	R	R	R
										R													
		R			R	R	R	R	R		**R**					R		R		R			
R		R		R	R	R	R	R	R	R	**R**	R	R	R	R	R	R	R	R	R			R
S		S		R	S		R			S				S	S			R	S	S			R
R	R	R	R	R	R	R	R	R	R	R			R	R	R	R	R	R	R	S	S	S	R
R	R	R		R	R	R	R	R	R	S	**R**	R	R	R	S	R		R	R	R			R
R	R	R	R	R	R	R	R	R	R		**R**	R	Y	R	R	R	R	R	R	R	R	R	R
R	R	R	R	R	R	R	R	R	R		**S**	R	R	R	R	R	R	R	R	R	R	R	R
		R	R	R	R	R		R	R	R	**R**	R			R		R		R	R			
R		R		R	R	R	R				**R**			R	R	R		R	R	R	R		R

Annex III.A: Selected multilateral agreements (worldwide) *(cont.)*

Y = in force   S = signed   R = ratified   D = denounced

		CAN	MEX	USA	JPN	KOR	AU	
1996 London	Amendment to convention	S						
1977 Geneva	Conv. – Protec. of workers against occup. hazards in the working env. due to air poll., noise and vibrat. (ILO 148)	Y						
1978 London	Protocol – Prevention of pollution from ships (MARPOL PROT)	Y	R	R	R	R	R	R
1978 London	Annex III	Y		R	R	R	R	R
1978 London	Annex IV				R			
1978 London	Annex V	Y		R	R	R	R	R
1997 London	Annex VI							
1979 Bonn	Conv. – Conservation of migratory species of wild animals	Y						R
1991 London	Agreem. – Conservation of bats in Europe	Y						
1992 New York	Agreem. – Conservation of small cetaceans of the Baltic and the North Seas (ASCOBANS)	Y						
1996 Monaco	Agreem. – Conservation of cetaceans of the Black Sea, Mediterranean Sea and Contiguous Atlantic Area							
1982 Montego Bay	Conv. – Law of the sea	Y	S	R		R	R	R
1994 New York	Agreem. – relating to the implementation of part XI of the convention	Y	S		S	R	R	R
1995 New York	Agreem. – Implementation of the provisions of the convention relating to the conservation and management of straddling fish stocks and highly migratory fish stocks	R		R	S	S	S	
1983 Geneva	Agreem. – Tropical timber	Y	R		R	R	R	R
1994 New York	Revised agreem. – Tropical timber	Y	R		R	R	R	
1985 Vienna	Conv. – Protection of the ozone layer	Y	R	R	R	R	R	R
1987 Montreal	Protocol (substances that deplete the ozone layer)	Y	R	R	R	R	R	R
1990 London	Amendment to protocol	Y	R	R	R	R	R	R
1992 Copenhagen	Amendment to protocol	Y	R	R	R	R	R	R
1997 Montreal	Amendment to protocol	Y	R				R	R
1986 Vienna	Conv. – Early notification of a nuclear accident	Y	R	R	R	R	R	R
1986 Vienna	Conv. – Assistance in the case of a nuclear accident or radiological emergency	Y	S	R	R	R	R	R
1989 Basel	Conv. – Control of transboundary movements of hazardous wastes and their disposal	Y	R	R	S	R	R	R
1995	Amendment							
1989 London	Conv. – Salvage	Y	R	R	R			R
1990 Geneva	Conv. – Safety in the use of chemicals at work (ILO 170)	Y	R					
1990 London	Conv. – Oil pollution preparedness, response and co-operation (OPRC)	Y	R	R	R	R		R
1992 Rio de Janeiro	Conv. – Biological diversity	Y	R	R	S	R	R	R
1992 New York	Conv. – Framework convention on climate change	Y	R	R	R	R	R	R
1997 Kyoto	Protocol	S	S	S	S	S	S	
1993 Paris	Conv. – Prohibition of the development, production, stockpiling and use of chemical weapons and their destruction	Y	R	R	S	R	S	R
1993 Geneva	Conv. – Prevention of major industrial accidents (ILO 174)	Y						
1993	Agreem. – Promote compliance with international conservation and management measures by fishing vessels on the high seas	R	R	R				
1994 Vienna	Conv. – Nuclear safety	Y	R	R	R	R	R	R
1994 Paris	Conv. – Combat desertification in those countries experiencing serious drought and/or desertification, particularly in Africa	Y	R	R	S	R	R	S
1996 London	Conv. – Liability and compensation for damage in connection with the carriage of hazardous and noxious substances by sea	S						

Annex III.A: *Selected multilateral agreements (worldwide) (cont.)*

Y = in force   S = signed   R = ratified   D = denounced

NZL	AUT	BEL	CZE	DNK	FIN	FRA	DEU	GRC	HUN	ISL	IRL	ITA	LUX	NLD	NOR	POL	PRT	ESP	SWE	CHE	TUR	UKD	EU
			S	S	S	S						S	S				S		S				
		R	R	R	R	R	R		R			R		R	R		R					R	
R	R	R	R	R	R	R	R	R	R	R	**R**	R	R	R	R	R	R	R	R	R	R	R	
R	R	R	R	R	R	R	R	R	R		**R**	R	R	R	R	R	R	R	R			R	
		R	R	R	R	R	R	R	R			R	R		R	R	R	R	R			R	
R	R	R	R	R	R	R	R	R	R	R	R	R	R	R	R	R	R	R	R	R	R	R	
													S					S					
	R	R	R	R	R	R	R		R		**R**	R	R	R	R	R	R	R	R	R		R	R
	S	R	R		S	R		R		**R**		R	R	R		S		R				R	
		S		R		S	R						R				R					R	S
				S		S			S				S	S			S			S			S
R	R	R	R	S	R	R	R	R	S	R	**R**	R	S	R	R	R	R	R	R	S		R	R
R	R	R	R	S	R	R	R	R		R	**R**	R	S	R	R	R	R	R	R	S		R	R
S	S	S		S	S	S	S	S		R	**S**	S	S	S	R		S	S	S			S	S
R	R	R		R	R	R	R	R		**R**	R	R	R		R		R	R	R	R		R	R
R	R	R		R	R	R	R	R		**R**	R	R		R		R	R	R	R	R		R	R
R	R	R	R	R	R	R	R	R	R	R	**R**	R	R	R	R	R	R	R	R	R	R	R	R
R	R	R	R	R	R	R	R	R	R	R	**R**	R	R	R	R	R	R	R	R	R	R	R	R
R	R	R	R	R	R	R	R	R	R	R	**R**	R	R	R	R	R	R	R	R	R	R	R	R
R	S			R		R		R				R		R			R	R					
R	R	R	R	R	R	R	R	R	R	R	**R**	R	S	R	R	R	R	R	R	R	R	R	
R	R	R	R	S	R	R	R	R	R	S	**R**	R		R	S	R	S	R	R	R	R	R	
R	R	R	R	R	R	R	R	R	R	R	**R**	R	R	R	R	R	R	R	R	R	R	R	R
	R	S		R	R							R		R			R	R				R	R
		R	S		S	R		R		**R**	R		R	R	S		S	R	R	R		R	
														R				R					
		R	R	R	R	R		R	**R**	R		R	R	S		R	R	R			R	
R	R	R	R	R	R	R	R	R	R	**R**	R	R	R	R	R	R	R	R	R	R	R	R
R	R	R	R	R	R	R	R	R	R	**R**	R	R	R	R	R	R	R	R	R		R	R
S	S	S	S	S	S	S	S	S		**S**	S	S	S	S	S	S	S	S			S	S
R	R	R	R	R	R	R	R	R	S	**R**	R	S	R	R	R	R	R	R	S	R	S	S
	S												R					R				
													R					R				R
	R	R	R	R	R	R	R	R	R	S	**R**	R	R	R	R	R	R	R	R	R	R	R
	R	R		R	R	R	R	R	R	R	**R**	R	R	R	R		R	R	R	R	R	R	R
			S	S		S						S	S				S					

Annex III.A: Selected multilateral agreements (worldwide) *(cont.)*
Y = in force   S = signed   R = ratified   D = denounced

		CAN	MEX	USA	JPN	KOR	AU
1996 The Hague	Agreem. – Conservation of African-Eurasian migratory waterbirds						
1997 Vienna	Conv. – Supplementary compensation for nuclear damage...			S			S
1997 Vienna	Conv. – Joint convention on the safety of spent fuel management and on the safety of radioactive waste management	R		S		S	S
1997 New York	Conv. – Law of the non-navigational uses of international watercourses						
1998 Rotterdam	Conv. – Prior informed consent procedure for hazardous chemicals and pesticides (PIC)			S	S	S	S

Source: IUCN; OECD.

Annex III.A: ***Selected multilateral agreements (worldwide)*** *(cont.)*

Y = in force   S = signed   R = ratified   D = denounced

NZL	AUT	BEL	CZE	DNK	FIN	FRA	DEU	GRC	HUN	ISL	**IRL**	ITA	LUX	NLD	NOR	POL	PRT	ESP	SWE	CHE	TUR	UKD	EU
		S					S		S		**S**			S									
			S									S											
	S	S	R	R	S	S	R	S	R		**S**	S	S	S	R	S		R	R	S		S	
				R			S		S				S		R		S						
S	S	S	S	S	S	S	S	S	S			S	S	S	S	S	S	S	S	S	S	S	S

Annex III.B: Selected multilateral agreements (regional)

Y = in force   S = signed   R = ratified   D = denounced

			CAN	MEX	USA	JPN	KOR	AU
1933	London	Conv. – Preservation of fauna and flora in their natural state	Y					
1946	London	Conv. – Regulation of the meshes of fishing nets and the size limits of fish...	Y					
1958	Dublin	Amendments	Y					
1960	London	Amendments	Y					
1961	Copenhagen	Amendments	Y					
1962	Hamburg	Amendments	Y					
1963	London	Amendments	Y					
1950	Paris	Conv. – Protection of birds...	Y					
1957	Geneva	Agreem. – International carriage of dangerous goods by road (ADR)	Y					
1975	New York	Protocol	Y					
1958	Geneva	Agreem. – Adoption of unif. cond. of approv. and recipr. recogn. of approv. for motor veh. equip. and parts	Y					
1959	Washington	Treaty – Antarctic...	Y	R		R	R	R	R
1991	Madrid	Protocol to the Antarctic treaty (environmental protection)...		S		S	S	S	R
1960	Paris	Conv. – Third party liability in the field of nuclear energy	Y					
1963	Brussels	Supplementary convention...	Y					
1964	Paris	Additional protocol to the convention...................................	Y					
1964	Paris	Additional protocol to the supplementary convention	Y					
1982	Brussels	Protocol amending the convention.......................................	Y					
1982	Brussels	Protocol amending the supplementary convention	Y					
1988	Vienna	Joint protocol relating to the application of the Vienna Convention and the Paris Convention...............................	Y					
1964	Brussels	Agreem. – Measures for the conservation of Antarctic Fauna and Flora	Y		R	R			R
1964	London	Conv. – Fisheries	Y					
1967	London	Conv. – Conduct of fishing operations in the North Atlantic ..	Y	S		S			
1968	Strasbourg	Agreem. – Restriction of the use of certain detergents in washing and cleaning products.....................................	Y					
1983	Strasbourg	Protocol..	Y					
1968	Paris	Conv. – Protection of animals during international transport	Y					
1979	Strasbourg	Protocol..	Y					
1969	London	Conv. – Protection of the archaeological heritage.................	Y					
1972	Oslo	Conv. – Prevention of marine pollution by dumping from ships and aircraft	Y					
1983		Protocol..	Y					
1972	London	Conv. – Conservation of Antarctic seals	Y	R		R	R		R
1973	Oslo	Agreem. – Conservation of polar bears	Y	R		R			
1974	Paris	Conv. – Prevention of marine pollution from land-based sources .	Y					
1986	Paris	Protocol..	Y					
1992	Paris	Conv. – Protection of North-East Atlantic marine env. (replace Oslo-1972 and Paris-1974)	Y					
1978	Ottawa	Conv. – Future multilateral co-operation in the Northwest Atlantic fisheries (NAFO)	Y	R			R	R	
1979	Bern	Conv. – Conservation of European wildlife and natural habitats...	Y					
1979	Geneva	Conv. – Long-range transboundary air pollution	Y	R		R			
1984	Geneva	Protocol (financing of EMEP)	Y	R		R			
1985	Helsinki	Protocol (reduction of sulphur emissions or their transboundary fluxes by at least 30%)............................	Y	R					

Annex III.B: Selected multilateral agreements (regional)

Y = in force   S = signed   R = ratified   D = denounced

NZL	AUT	BEL	CZE	DNK	FIN	FRA	DEU	GRC	HUN	ISL	IRL	ITA	LUX	NLD	NOR	POL	PRT	ESP	SWE	CHE	TUR	UKD	EU
	R					S						R						S	R				R
	R	R		R	R	R				R	**R**			R	R		R	R	R				R
	R	R		R	R	R				R	**R**			R	R	R	R	R	R				R
	R	R		R	R	R				R	**R**			R	R	R	R	R	R				R
	R	R		R	R	R				R	**R**			R	R	R	R	R	R				R
	R	R		R	R	R				R	**R**			R	R	R	R	R	R				R
	R	R		R	R	R				R	**R**			R	R	R	R	R	R				R
	S	R		S		S				R		R	R	R				S	R	R	R	R	
	R	R	R	R	R	R	R	R	R			R	R	R	R	R	R	R	R	R			R
	R	R		R	R	R	R		R			R	R	R	R	R	R	R	R	R			R
	R	R	R	R	R	R	R		R			R	R	R	R	R	R	R	R	R			R
R	R	R	R	R	R	R	R	R	R			R		R	R	R		R	R	R	R		R
R	S	S	S	S	R	R	S	R	S			S		S	S	S		R	R	S			S
	S	R		R	R	R	R					R	S	R	R		R	R	R	S	R		R
	S	R		R	R	R	R					R	S	R	R			R	R	S			R
	S	R		R	R	R	R	R				R	S	R	R		R	R	R	S	R		R
	S	R		R	R	R	R					R	S	R	R			R	R	S			R
	S	R		R	R	R	R	R				R	S	R	R		R	R	R	S	R		R
	S	R		R	R	R	R					R	S	R	R			R	R	S			R
	S	R		R	R	R	R					R	S	R	R			R	R	S			R
	S	R		S	R	R	S	R				R		R	R	R	S	S	R	S	S	S	S
R	R			R								R			R	R							R
	R			R	R	R					**R**	R	S	R		R	R	R	R				R
	R			R	R					R	**S**	R		R	R	S	R	R	R				R
	R			R		R	R					R	R	R				R		R		R		R
	R			R		S						R	R	R				R		S				R
R	R		R	R	R	R	R			R	**R**	R	R	R	R		R	R	R	R	R	R	
R	R		R	R	R	R	R			R	**R**	R	R	R	R		R	R	R	R			
R	R			R	R	R	R			R		R	R				R	R	R	R			
	R			R	R	R	R			R	**R**			R	R		R	R	R	R				R
	R			R	R	R	R			R	**R**			R	R		R	R	R	R				R
S	R				R	R						R			R	R	R							R
	R		R												R									
	R			R	R	R				R	**R**		S	R	R		R	R	R			R	R
	R			R	R	R				R	**R**			R	R		R	R	R			R	R
	R			R	R	R	R			R	**R**			R	R		R	R	R	R		R	R
		R								R				R	R	D	D							R
R	R	R	R	R	R	R	R	R	R	R	**R**	R	R	R	R	R	R	R	R	R	R	R	R
R	R	R	R	R	R	R	R	R	R	R	**R**	R	R	R	R	R	R	R	R	R	R	R	R
R	R	R	R	R	R	R	R	R			**R**	R	R	R	R	R	R	R	R	R	R	R	R
	R	R	R	R	R	R	R		R			R	R	R	R					R	R		

© OECD 2000

Annex III.B: Selected multilateral agreements (regional) (cont.)

Y = in force S = signed R = ratified D = denounced

		CAN	MEX	USA	JPN	KOR	AUS
1988 Sofia	Protocol (control of emissions of nitrogen oxides or their transboundary fluxes)	Y	R	R			
1991 Geneva	Protocol (control of emissions of volatile organic compounds or their transboundary fluxes)	Y	S	S			
1994 Oslo	Protocol (further reduction of sulphur emissions)	Y	R				
1998 Aarhus	Protocol (heavy metals)		R	S			
1998 Aarhus	Protocol (persistent organic pollutants)		R	S			
1999 Gothenburg	Protocol (abate acidification, eutrophication and ground-level ozone)		S	S			
1980 Madrid	Conv. – Transfrontier co-operation between territorial communities or authorities	Y					
1995 Strasbourg	Additional protocol	Y					
1998 Strasbourg	Second protocol						
1980 Canberra	Conv. – Conservation of Antarctic marine living resources	Y	R	R	R	R	R
1980 Bern	Conv. – International carriage of dangerous goods by train (COTIF)						
1980 London	Conv. – Multilateral co-operation in North-East Atlantic fisheries	Y					
1982 Paris	Memorandum of understanding on port state control	Y					
1982 Reykjavik	Conv. – Conservation of salmon in the North Atlantic Ocean.	Y	R	R			
1983 Bonn	Agreem. – Co-operation in dealing with pollution of the North Sea by oil and other harmful subst.	Y					
1989 Bonn	Amendment	Y					
1989 Geneva	Conv. – Civil liab. for damage caused during carriage of dang. goods by road, rail, and inland navig. (CRTD)						
1991 Espoo	Conv. – Environmental impact assessment in a transboundary context	Y	R	S			
1992 Helsinki	Conv. – Transboundary effects of industrial accidents		S	S			
1992 Nuuk	Agreem. – Co-operation on research, conservation and management of marine mammals in the North Atlantic						
1992 Helsinki	Conv. – Protection and use of transboundary water courses and international lakes	Y					
1992 La Valette	European Conv. – Protection of the archaeological heritage (revised)	Y					
1992 Vienna	Agreem. – Forecast, prevention and mitigation of natural and technological disasters						S
1993 Lugano	Conv. – Civil liability for damage resulting from activities dangerous to the environment						
1994 Lisbon	Treaty – Energy Charter	Y				S	S
1994 Lisbon	Protocol (energy efficiency and related environmental aspects).	Y				S	S
1998 Aarhus	Conv. – Access to environmental information and public participation in environmental decision-making						
1998 Strasbourg	Conv. – Protection of the environment through criminal law.						

Source: IUCN; OECD.

Annex III.B: *Selected multilateral agreements (regional)* (cont.)

Y = in force   S = signed   R = ratified   D = denounced

NZL	AUT	BEL	CZE	DNK	FIN	FRA	DEU	GRC	HUN	ISL	IRL	ITA	LUX	NLD	NOR	POL	PRT	ESP	SWE	CHE	TUR	UKD	EU
	R	S	R	R	R	R	R	R	R		**R**	R	R	R	R	S		R	R	R		R	R
	R	S	R	R	R	R	R	R	S			R	R	R	R		S	R	R	R		R	S
	R	S	R	R	R	R	R	R	S		**R**	R	R	R	R	S		R	R	R		R	R
	S	S	S	S	S	S	S	S	S	S	**S**	S	S	S	S	S	S	S	S	S		S	S
	S	S	S	S	S	S	S	S	S	S	**S**	S	S	S	S	S	S	S	S	S		S	S
	S	S	S	S	S	S	S	S	S		**S**	S	S	S	S			S	S	S	S		
	R	R	R	R	R	R	R		R	S	**R**	R	R	R	R	R	R	R	R	R	R	S	
	S					R	R			S				R	R			S		R	R			
R		R			R	R	R	R					R		R	R	R		R	R			R	R
						R																		
			R							R					R	R	R	R	R					R
		R		R	R	R	R			R		**R**	R		R	R	R	R	R				R	
		R	R							R					R				R					R
		R		R		R	R								R	R				R		R	R
		R		R		R	R								R	R				R		R	R
						S																	
	R	R	S	R	R	S	S	R	R	S	**S**	R	R	R	R	R	S	R	R	R		R	R
	R	S		S	S	S	R	R	R			S	R	S	R	S	S	R	S	R		S	R
								S								S							
	R	S			R	R	R	R	R			R	R	R	S	R	S	R	R			S	R
			S	S	R	R	S	S	R		**R**	S	S	S	R	R	R	S	R	R	R	S	S
							S				S		S				S						
				S			S		S			S	S	S			S						
	R	R	R	R	R	R	R	R	S	**R**	R	R	R	S	S	R	R	R	R	R	S	R	R
	R	R	R	R	R	R	R	R	S	**R**	R	R	R	S	S	R	R	R	R	R	S	R	R
	S	S	S	S	S	S	S	S	S	**S**	S	S	S	S	S	S	S	S	S	S		S	S
	S	S		S	S	S	S		S			S								S				

Annex IV

CHRONOLOGY OF SELECTED ENVIRONMENTAL EVENTS (1990-99)

1990

- Environment Action Programme includes commitments to invest IEP 1 billion in environmental infrastructure by 2000 and to establish Environmental Protection Agency.
- Sale of bituminous solid fuel prohibited in Dublin following episodes of severe winter smog.
- Dublin Declaration, a European Community policy statement on global environmental issues, adopted by European Council.
- Local Government (Water Pollution) (Amendment) Act strengthens water pollution legislation.
- Local Government (Planning and Development) Act consolidates planning legislation in relation to compensation.
- Derelict Sites Act strengthens powers to prevent dereliction.
- Environmental information centre (ENFO) of the Department of the Environment and Local Government (DOELG) provides authoritative public information on the environment.

1991

- Temple Bar designated Dublin cultural quarter.
- Plan for Social Housing to control construction of estates on peripheral greenfield sites.
- First comprehensive report on Quality of Drinking Water in Ireland published by DOELG.
- Sea Pollution Act strengthens protection of marine environment from ships' pollution, allowing Ireland to become a contracting party to two international treaties.
- Creation of National Parks and Wildlife Service under Office of Public Works.
- Creation of Burren and Wicklow Mountain National Parks.
- Creation of a Whale and Dolphin Sanctuary – the first in Europe.

1992

- UN Conference on Water and the Environment in Dublin, as part of UNCED preparations.
- Ireland's National Report to UNCED published by DOELG.
- Creation of Marine Institute to provide research support to relevant Government Departments.

- Creation of Radiological Protection Institute to address risks associated with radioactive materials.
- National Emergency Plan for Nuclear Accidents published by Department of Energy.
- Environmental Protection Agency Act passed.
- Studies on Implications of Climate Change for Ireland published by DOELG.

1993

- Creation of Environmental Protection Agency (EPA) to perform integrated licensing of certain industrial and other activities, monitor and report on environmental quality, assist public authorities with environmental protection functions, and promote and co-ordinate environmental research.
- Comprehensive report on Water Quality in Ireland 1987-90 published by DOELG.
- Green 2000 Advisory Group stresses relationship between environmental protection and economic and social development.
- Access to Information on the Environment Regulations give the public new statutory rights to obtain environmental information held by Irish public authorities, giving effect to Directive 90/313/EEC.
- Local Government (Planning and Development) Act applies physical planning requirements to State authorities, except in limited cases relating to public safety, national security, etc.
- Ireland's first commercial windfarm at Bellacorrick, Co. Mayo, with capacity of 6.45 MW.
- Commissioning of natural gas interconnector between Ireland and the UK.

1994

- Integrated Pollution Control (IPC) licensing by EPA starts.
- National Development Plan 1994-99 includes commitments to invest IEP 605 million in water and sewerage services. The second Community Support Framework for Ireland sets out joint Irish-European development priorities for 1994-99.
- Environmental Services Operational Programme 1994-99 provides for investment in water services, waste management, coastal protection, group water schemes and research and development.
- Ireland receives aid under EU Cohesion Fund, for the first time, to assist in developing water and sewerage infrastructure.
- New schemes for Control of Farmyard Pollution and Rural Environmental Protection.
- Urban Renewal Scheme 1994-97 marks a major shift away from office and commercial development towards refurbishment and conservation.
- Creation of Irish Energy Centre (IEC) to co-ordinate national energy efficiency and renewable energy policy.
- Recycling for Ireland, national strategy for recycling municipal waste, published by DOELG.

• Creation of Green (later called Environmental) Network of Government Departments, chaired by DOELG, to improve co-ordination between environment units.

1995

• Moving Towards Sustainability, review of recent environmental policy and developments, published by DOELG.
• Local Agenda 21 launched by DOELG with publication of Local Authorities and Sustainable Development: Guidelines on Local Agenda 21.
• Dublin Transportation Initiative (DTI) report on integrated transport policy.
• EPA co-ordinates major investigation of animal health problems on two farms in Co. Limerick.
• EU Eco-Management and Audit Scheme (EMAS) launched in Ireland.
• Ban on sale of bituminous solid fuel extended to Cork.
• Ministerial Committee on Nuclear Safety co-ordinates actions on Sellafield and the Irish Sea.
• Erne Nutrient Management Scheme introduced.
• Car scrappage scheme introduced, allowing IEP 1 000 of new vehicle registration tax to be refunded when cars over ten years old are scrapped.
• Creation of Heritage Council under the Heritage Act.
• Details of proposed Natural Heritage Areas published.

1996

• Waste Management Act extends EPA functions to include licensing of new and existing large-scale waste disposal facilities. The Act also requires farmers to prepare nutrient management plans in the interests of water quality protection.
• First National Waste Database Report and first State of the Environment Report published by EPA.
• Green Government Guide published by DOELG to advise Government Departments and Agencies on best environmental management practices.
• Crude oil washed up on south and south-east coasts from the Sea Empress.
• Code of Good Agricultural Practice to Protect Waters from Pollution by Nitrates published by DOELG and Department of Agriculture and Food.
• National Biodiversity Plan published by Department of Arts, Heritage, Gaeltacht and the Islands (DAHGI) as a discussion paper.
• Integrated Pollution Control (IPC) licensing for new intensive agricultural activities by EPA.
• Grant schemes to promote recycling *infra*structure and development of waste management strategies by private sector and local authorities.

1997

- Sustainable Development: A Strategy for Ireland constitutes national policy on sustainable development.
- Environmental Partnership Fund launched by DOELG with initial annual budget of IEP 100 000.
- Litter Pollution Act strengthens powers of local authorities.
- Water Quality in Ireland 1991-94 published by EPA.
- DOELG launches Managing Ireland's Rivers and Lakes – A Catchment-Based Strategy against Eutrophication in response to increasing eutrophication in rivers and lakes.
- Lough Derg and Lough Ree Catchment Monitoring and Management Systems launched as part of major investment programme in sewerage infrastructure.
- Water Quality Management Strategy Reports for the Erne and Foyle Catchments published by DOELG and the Department of the Environment in Northern Ireland, under EU INTERREG initiative.
- Coastal Zone Management – A Draft Policy for Ireland published as discussion document.
- Urban Waste Water Discharges in Ireland in 1994 and 1995, first report on sewage treatment facilities in Ireland, published by EPA.
- Dublin Docklands Development Authority (DDDA) established for dockland redevelopment.
- European Communities (Natural Habitats) Regulations initiate process of designating Special Areas of Conservation.
- Packaging Waste Regulations and Farm Plastics Regulations require producers of packaging/farm plastics to take steps to recover/recycle these waste streams. Two voluntary initiatives introduced: REPAK scheme for packaging waste recovery, and Farm Plastic Films Recovery Scheme involving industry and farmers.
- Aer Rianta (Dublin Airport) meets international environmental management standard (ISO 14001), becoming first airport in world to do so.
- Grant schemes to assist provision of hazardous waste infrastructure by private sector.

1998

- Limitation and Reduction of CO_2 and other Greenhouse Gases in Ireland published by DOELG and Department of Public Enterprise, followed by workshop on how to develop National Greenhouse Gas Abatement Strategy.
- Ban on sale of bituminous solid fuel extended to five additional towns/cities.
- Creation of national and regional networks of Local Agenda 21 officers.
- Creation of Mayo National Park.
- Short-Term Action Plan published by Dublin Transportation Office to ease traffic congestion, pending completion of major infrastructure projects.
- Nutrient Management Guidelines for local authorities issued by DOELG.
- Monitoring and management system for Lough Leane Catchment (Co. Kerry) to address severe algal bloom problems.

- Quality of Bathing Waters (Amendment) Regulations to cover 130 bathing areas.
- Environmental cross-compliance introduced by Department of Agriculture and Food in granting ewe premia to farmers using common lands in Counties Kerry, Galway, Mayo, Sligo, Leitrim and Donegal.
- Tax relief for corporate investments to encourage development of renewable energy sources such as wind energy and biomass.
- Genetically Modified Organisms and the Environment issued by DOELG as public consultation paper.
- Transport, treatment and disposal of hazardous clinical/healthcare waste organised through contractor appointed jointly by health authorities in Ireland and Northern Ireland.
- Changing our Ways, policy statement on waste management, published by DOELG.
- Contract awarded for private car testing system in Ireland.

1999

- Creation of National Sustainable Development Partnership (Comhar), with broad representation from across Irish society, as forum for national consultation and dialogue on all issues surrounding pursuit of sustainable development.
- First national report on a key set of environmental indicators published by EPA.
- National Budget includes tax concessions in transport sector to promote construction of park and ride facilities in urban areas, provision of bus and rail passes to employees and purchase of small cars.
- Local Government (Planning and Development) Act extends planning control system to protect architectural heritage.
- Planning and Development Bill aims to revise and consolidate planning legislation and formally introduce sustainable development as objective in Irish planning system.
- Strategic Planning Guidelines for Greater Dublin Area published jointly by local and regional authorities and DOELG.
- Guidelines for Planning Authorities on Residential Density published by DOELG to increase supply of housing from existing land and infrastructure, to make more economical use of infrastructure, and to improve environment and quality of life by reducing need to travel.
- Water Quality in Ireland 1995-97 published by EPA.
- Three Rivers Project (Rivers Boyne, Liffey and Suir) launched, providing major catchment based water quality monitoring and management initiative supported by EU Cohesion Fund.
- Guidelines to assist local authorities developing Groundwater Protection Schemes jointly prepared by EPA, Geological Survey of Ireland and DOELG.
- Ireland's Marine and Coastal Areas and Adjacent Seas: An Environmental Assessment published by Marine Institute.
- Wildlife (Amendment) Bill published by DAHGI to improve national wildlife legislation and bring it in line with international conservation practice.
- New Sustainable Building Awards Scheme launched by DOELG.

- Urban Renewal Scheme includes Integrated Area Plan with time horizon of 2002.
- Proposed National Hazardous Waste Management Plan published by EPA for public consultation.
- Public investment of IEP 70 million to upgrade Whitegate Refinery to meet EU Auto Oil programme fuel specifications.
- National policy position on Genetically Modified Organisms and the Environment issued by DOELG following public consultation debate.
- Green Paper on Sustainable Energy published by Department of Public Enterprise.
- Eco-audit system for Government plans/policies introduced on a pilot basis.
- Major environmental awareness campaign launched by DOELG.
- National Development Plan 2000-06 provides for substantial investment in environmental infrastructure.

OECD PUBLICATIONS, 2, rue André-Pascal, 75775 PARIS CEDEX 16
PRINTED IN FRANCE
(97 2000 06 1 P) ISBN 92-64-18292-6 – No. 51461 2000